"If you think racial reconciliation for Christians is easy, this book will convince you otherwise. It takes the reader on a complex journey from 'whiteness' into the arms of a 'black Jesus' who offers hope for a better world."

— TONY CAMPOLO, PhD, Eastern University

"The author, a Southern white, traces his pilgrimages into the black community and black church. Though profoundly grateful for his experiences and acceptance into the beloved community, Wilson-Hartgrove is also keenly aware of the damage racism has done to both the black and white communities. This book is written with much wisdom and honesty."

— DR. JOHN M. PERKINS, Foundation for Reconciliation and Development

NAVPRESS DELIBERATE

From the very beginning, God created humans to love Him and each other. He intended for His people to be a blessing to everyone on earth so that everyone would know Him (Genesis 12:2). Jesus also taught this over and over and promised to give His people all they needed to make it happen — His resources, His power, and His presence (Matthew 28:20; John 14:12-14). NavPress Deliberate takes Him at His word and stirs its readers to do the same — to be the children of God for whom creation is groaning to be revealed. We have only to glance through the Bible to discover what it looks like to be the blessing God has intended: caring for the poor, orphan, widow, prisoner, and foreigner (Micah 6:8; Matthew 25:31-46; Isaiah 58); and redeeming the world — everyone and everything in it (Colossians 1:19-20; Romans 8:19-23).

NavPress Deliberate encourages readers to embrace this holistic and vibrant Christian faith: It is both contemplative and active; it unites mystery-embracing faith with theological rootedness; it breaks down the sacred/secular divide, recognizing God's sovereignty and redemptive work in every facet of life; it dialogues with other faiths and worldviews and embraces God's truth found there; it creates culture and uses artistic ability to unflinchingly tell the truth about this life and God's redemption of it; it fosters a faith bold enough to incarnate the gospel in a shrinking and diverse world. NavPress Deliberate is for everyone on a pilgrimage to become like Jesus and to continue His work of living and discipling among all people.

Become what you believe.
The NavPress Deliberate Team

FREE TO
BE BOUND

CHURCH BEYOND THE COLOR LINE

JONATHAN WILSON-HARTGROVE

NAVPRESS

OUR GUARANTEE TO YOU

We believe so strongly in the message of our books that we are making this quality guarantee to you. If for any reason you are disappointed with the content of this book, return the title page to us with your name and address and we will refund to you the list price of the book. To help us serve you better, please briefly describe why you were disappointed. Mail your refund request to: NavPress, P.O. Box 35002, Colorado Springs, CO 80935.

For a free catalog
of NavPress books & Bible studies call
1-800-366-7788 (USA) or 1-800-839-4769 (Canada).

www.navpress.com

The Navigators is an international Christian organization. Our mission is to advance the gospel of Jesus and His kingdom into the nations through spiritual generations of laborers living and discipling among the lost. We see a vital movement of the gospel, fueled by prevailing prayer, flowing freely through relational networks and out into the nations where workers for the kingdom are next door to everywhere.

NavPress is the publishing ministry of The Navigators. The mission of NavPress is to reach, disciple, and equip people to know Christ and make Him known by publishing life-related materials that are biblically rooted and culturally relevant. Our vision is to stimulate spiritual transformation through every product we publish.

ISBN-13: 978-1-60006-190-5
ISBN-10: 1-60006-190-7

Cover design by studiogearbox.com
Cover image credits:
Neon church cross — Keith Goldstein/ Photonica
Church sign image — Chris Gilbert/Gearbox
Image of churchgoers holding hands — M. Lester/PonkaWonka.com
Creative Team: Don Simpson, Cara Iverson, Darla Hightower, Arvid Wallen, Kathy Guist

Some of the anecdotal illustrations in this book are true to life and are included with the permission of the persons involved. All other illustrations are composites of real situations, and any resemblance to people living or dead is coincidental.

Unless otherwise identified, all Scripture quotations in this publication are taken from the HOLY BIBLE: NEW INTERNATIONAL VERSION* (NIV*). Copyright © 1973, 1978, 1984 by International Bible Society. Used by permission of Zondervan Publishing House. All rights reserved. Other versions used include: the *King James Version* (KJV).

Library of Congress Cataloging-in-Publication Data

Wilson-Hartgrove, Jonathan, 1980-
  Free to be bound : church beyond the color line / Jonathan
Wilson-Hartgrove.
      p. cm.
  Includes bibliographical references.
  ISBN 978-1-60006-190-5
  1. United States--Church history. 2. Race--Religious
aspects--Christianity. 3. Reconciliation--Religious
aspects--Christianity. I. Title.
BR517.W54 2008
277.3'083089--dc22

                              2007044509

Printed in the United States of America

1 2 3 4 5 6 7 8 / 12 11 10 09 08

For Robert and Kathleen Daniels

Contents

Foreword   11

Preface   15

Hearing the Gospel in a New Key

Chapter 1: I'll Fly Away   23

Chapter 2: If It Had Not Been for the Lord   35

Chapter 3: I Need You, You Need Me   55

Crossing over Jordan

Chapter 4: Nobody Knows but Jesus   77

Chapter 5: I Want Jesus to Walk with Me   95

Chapter 6: I Know It Was the Blood   117

Blessed Be the Tie That Binds

Chapter 7: Climbing Jacob's Ladder   141

Chapter 8: The Whole World in His Hands   163

Chapter 9: No More Chains Holding Me   183

Discussion Guide   193

Notes   199

Author   205

Foreword

All Christians have a story to tell. It's a part of our witness to what God is actually doing in our own lives, of how He leads us and guides us from day to day. Jonathan Wilson-Hartgrove's story is one that needs to be told for all to hear. His is a story of growth and development and how we learn from each other, but in particular, how we are able to listen and affirm the dignity of who we are serving and learn from them.

Jonathan's story sort of reflects what we at the Christian Community Development Association (CCDA), and I in particular, believe about the way we learn, grow, and release the power of God through our lives. His life reflects the little Chinese proverb we use at CCDA, which says:

Go to the people
Live among them

Learn from them
Love them
Start with what they know
Build on what they have
The best leaders, when their work is finished
Their task is done
The people need to say 'we have done it ourselves.'

I believe this, in essence, is the key in leadership, the key to empowering people, and the key to our continued learning from people. Jonathan lived this proverb as he made his remarkable journey in search of truth. Here's one of our bright young scholar activists who happens to be a great writer. His keen mind led him to search for truth in a way that went deeper than most people's search for truth. Most people are content to stay within their comfortable cultural or church setting, trying to find truth within that setting. But Jonathan's search took him across racial and cultural barriers and from the white South and its limitations. He had to make the pilgrimage into the black community and the black church to discover truths that were missing from his previous church background. He then ended up not only attending an Afro-American church, but living in an Afro-American community.

Though profoundly grateful for his experiences and acceptance into the beloved community, Jonathan is also keenly aware of the damage racism has done to both the black and the white communities. The black church is a reflection of and a protest against white church oppression. The white church, on the other hand, has continued to try to bring its good theology to us to bring credibility to its history without adequately confessing that it was a church of oppression. The white church sort of rejected the black church in its progress, and the black church, because it was born out of that, sort of accepts the people who come to them.

Many white folks who come to the black community see that missing side. They discover that because our church was developed to protest the rejection and oppression of the white church, it's easy for the black church to accept whites into its society. What Jonathan learned during his journey was that his church, the white church, was a part of that oppression and that the black church was a part of the friend element within the society. So, here in America you have the church, the so-called black and white church. Maybe somewhere down the line we will find some truth in that. And maybe that's what fascinates Jonathan's search for truth.

Jonathan's search took him to a black church, where he now worships, and into an interracial community, where he now lives. It's easy for whites to see the black church as final just because it's better than the white church. I don't accept the black church as finality. It might be better than the white church in some ways, but it's not the best that God can do. That's not the church He built. He didn't build a church that had to come out of protest. He wants to build a church that comes out of His love.

Jonathan expresses this in this wonderfully written personal testimony. It's a story that's a must read for anyone who has an interest in reconciliation and becoming the church God wants us to be.

JOHN PERKINS,
COFOUNDER OF THE CHRISTIAN COMMUNITY DEVELOPMENT
ASSOCIATION

Preface

Lest you buy this book, read all the way to the end, and find yourself disappointed, wondering if NavPress really sticks to that money-back guarantee, I thought I'd tell you right at the start that this is not a how-to book on racial reconciliation. I've read a few of those books, and I'm sure you can find one if a how-to guide is what you want. But this is not it.

This is, instead, a how-it's-been book. It's a story—or, rather, a collection of stories—written along the way by a white boy who followed Jesus from Klan country to the black church, listening for the music that could teach his soul to sing. I decided to write this book because I found all those how-to books lacking. Not that they were wrong; I just wanted more. Slowly but surely, stumbling as I went, I learned to clap on two and four. I meditated on the wisdom of the spirituals—the truth deep down in the words and in the music. In time, I found myself whispering as I went about my work, "I will trust in the Lord / I will trust in the Lord 'til I die. . . ." I'm not there yet, but I hope one day that my whole life might become that song.

Scholars of American Christianity used to say that we couldn't really know much about the theology of slave churches because the people in them were uneducated and didn't write anything down. This was more or less accepted until the great Albert J. Raboteau noted in his monumental work *Slave Religion* that the theology of the slave church had been passed down in its songs. Without focusing so much on the theology, W.E.B. DuBois had already noted in his *Souls of Black Folk* that the deep wisdom of the Afro-American tradition is in its song. They are its gift to the world.

This book assumes that God's clearest self-revelation on the ground we call America is in the great songs of the black church tradition. Starting there, I've tried to hear what God is saying in those songs and follow where the Spirit leads. Looking back, I see three signposts that I've passed so far along the way. They give me some sense of where I've been and where I'm going. In keeping with them, I've divided this book into three sections.

The first is about how I came to hear the gospel in a new key through the voice of Rev. William Barber (who is, I have to say, still the best preacher I've ever heard). What I heard was not always easy, but I know now that it was good. It helped me see that I couldn't know Jesus without listening to the black church. Which led, as all stories must, to the next chapter—a second signpost marked "crossing over Jordan." I knew I had to join the black church to know Jesus more fully. So, together with my wife, Leah, I started worshipping at St. John's Baptist Church. Embraced by a new family, we've continued on the endless journey into God's love with our brothers and sisters here. They have become our teachers, mentors, companions, and fellow-travelers.

Conversations have led to conversions, many of which are not finished yet. But at some point we reached another signpost, and I realized I was bound to these people. In our life together, I learned to imagine possibilities I couldn't have dreamed of before. And I knew the tie that binds us to be a blessing.

In the Civil Rights Movement of the 1950s and 60s, America glimpsed the transformational power of the black church tradition in the assertion that human beings are bound to be free. The good news that message brought was clear not only in the dignity it restored to black Americans, but also in the hope it inspired in nonviolent freedom movements around the world. Forty years later, though, the hope of human brotherhood via civil rights has faded. Young black folks on city streets and in prison cells have grown cynical about the promises of citizenship. Afraid of crime and terrorism, most white Americans want safety more than any abstract notion of brotherhood. Maybe we are bound to be free, but free for what?

If this story has any single point to make, it is the quiet gospel hope that says we are *free to be bound together in Jesus Christ.* The liberating message of black Christianity need not lead to middle-class mediocrity or nihilistic violence. Instead, the New Testament vision of beloved community offers a radically alternative form of social life. If American Christians are to learn this way of living, we'll have to draw deeply from the wisdom of the black church. If we are to actually live it, we'll have to be changed into the sort of people who can live together across the modern construct that DuBois dubbed "the color line."

A book like this can't be imagined — even less written — without the help of innumerable people. Some of them you'll meet in the coming pages. But I want to take this chance to say how grateful I am for each of them. For the sake of protecting their trust,

I've changed the names of people whose conversations with me weren't already public. They need not be troubled by my attempts to say what I have learned from them.

A few debts should be named here, though, because their magnitude may not be clear otherwise. I couldn't have made the sense I have of the life I've lived if I hadn't had the chance to study with Willie Jennings and Jay Carter at Duke Divinity School. To the extent that I'm "doing theology" in this book, I'm doing a riff on the masterful work these two fine scholars have done (and they have only just begun). I must say that their scholarship is not separate from the community life they share at Mt. Level Baptist Church, under the leadership of Dr. William C. Turner, an exceptional pastor-theologian in his own right. Thirty years from now, I suspect it will be clear in American theology that there was a Mt. Level School at the beginning of the twenty-first century. I'm glad to have been one of its students.

I've had numerous other teachers whose wisdom runs deep, even if their teaching will not be remembered by historians of American theology. I'm still studying under Ann Atwater, my mother in the faith and in the movement. Thanks for everything, Grandma Ann. My deepest thanks also to Peanut, Abura, Carolyn, Wallace, Roy, Ms. Mecie, Peaches, Miya, Nora, Alvin, Barbara, Vern, Sylvia, Chanequa, and Bahari, all of whom have loved a white brother and helped me hear the good news that I've tried to share in this book. To all the saints at St. John's, thank you for adopting us into your family — and putting up with all the issues that came with us. To my neighbors in Walltown, thanks for sticking together through so many years and becoming such a fine community.

I owe a huge debt of gratitude also to the people who made it possible for me to write this story. To Chris, Emmanuel, Lauren,

John, and Tim: thanks for encouraging this project when it was just getting started. Thanks to Jesse for your careful read, helpful feedback, and beautiful life. And thanks to Tim for not only reading, but daring to trust that some of what I've said might be true. All the folks at Rutba bore with my absences and, grace upon grace, tolerated my presence as I tried to make sense of race and the church while living life. As they know all too well, I live by God's grace and theirs.

A huge thanks to all the good folks at NavPress who've worked hard to take electronic files from my computer and turn them into the book you're holding now. Thanks especially to Don Simpson—a sensitive eye who believed in the message and worked to make it clearer.

Leah, I love you and hope some day to write as gracefully as you live.

This book is dedicated to Rev. Robert and Kathleen Daniels, two servants who have toiled long in the Lord's vineyard, doing the sort of theology that teaches the soul to sing.

HEARING THE GOSPEL IN A NEW KEY

Though I knew that American racism had put blacks and whites into the roles of oppressors and oppressed, I had not experienced it as a victory for the oppressor. I knew well that racism had caused pain to black people, but I knew too that it had been a cause of pain to white people—it had been a cause of pain to me—and not just because of guilt. I knew that for white people it had involved loss and spiritual disfigurement. And I knew, from my own experience, that it had involved love.

Wendell Berry, *The Hidden Wound*

ONE

I'll Fly Away

The truest part of church is always the part you take home with you. For my family, it was the music. Sure, we had the occasional conversation, between bites of fried chicken and corn bread, about the preacher's sermon or the Sunday school lesson. And sometimes we would argue with Scripture like the rabbis who answer the claims of one verse with the contrasting view of another. (Mom: "You know the Bible says, 'Spare the rod and spoil the child.'" My brother: "I guess that means I'll have to turn the other cheek.") But my good Southern Baptist family never spent much time together without Nana making her way to the piano, Pa picking up his guitar, and Granny asking us to sing her favorite song, "I'll Fly Away."

Ours is a family that sings its faith. Granny led the choir at the Woodland Baptist Church in Mt. Airy, North Carolina, until she broke her ankle and had to move to King, North Carolina, to be closer to the rest of the family. Pa, her guitar-playing son,

met Nana when he was singing with a quartet at the Grapevine
Baptist Church, where her father was the pastor. Nana played the
piano there. She and Pa married and had three daughters. My
mom, the oldest, learned to play the bass. Her sister Leah took up
the drums. The youngest girl, Debra, was a singer from the start.
So the Cockerham family became Daybreak, a southern gospel
band. And I grew up listening to songs like "Canaan Land Is Just
in Sight" and "Just a Closer Walk with Thee."

I remember an afternoon at the county hospital where Granny
had been taken in for chest pains. The family was gathered around
her bed and had been briefed on what the doctors said. We asked
a few questions. We shuffled our feet. There wasn't much more
to say, so there we stood, waiting. The TV flickered overhead,
its sound muted out of respect for our time together. There was
a silence that begged to be filled, and right there on the cardiac
care unit of the Forsyth County Memorial Hospital, we started
singing Granny's favorite song.

Some glad morning when this life is over, I'll fly away . . .

For all we knew, we were singing about a day that might come
soon for Granny. She was by then already in her midseventies.
The Bible says three score and ten is a full life. Seventy years, and
then you fly away. With enough practice, I guess, it becomes the
sort of thing you can sing about, even in a hospital room.

When I die, hallelujah by and by, I'll fly away.

We sang that hope together with Granny, and I knew that it
was true. Someday she would fly away to "God's celestial shore."
Someday I would fly away too.

By the time I was fifteen, I was itching to get away from King,
North Carolina. My world of dirt roads, church songs, homemade
ice cream, and Sunday school seemed too small. Filled with a restless energy that seemed to spring up together with the hair in my

armpits, I became a teenage snob. The books I read at school gave me language that I used to set myself apart from the "common" people who were my neighbors and cousins, pastors and friends. In my head I started to correct the deacon of the week's grammar during his offertory prayer. Week to week I listened to our preacher read a text and then say what I thought was the same thing he had said the week before. (I had not yet heard the great Swiss theologian Karl Barth's dictum, "We can only repeat ourselves," but if I had, I suspect I would have just thought he was wrong.) By the ripe old age of fifteen I had convinced myself that I was ready for some higher form of Christianity. Surely there had to be more to church than sitting around for seventy years waiting for everyone else to get saved so we could all fly away to glory. I wanted a Jesus who said something new.

So I sharpened my critical skills, reading everything I could find to help me say what was wrong with the church. Reason promised to lift me high above the simplistic faith of Granny's song. I began to suspect that her desire to "fly away" was rooted in an otherworldly religion that neglected responsibility in the real world. I didn't want wings for my spirit—I wanted a ticket on US Airways. I had places to go in this world. And I wanted to make a difference.

So I turned my hope to politics. Not a politics without God, though. Religion and politics were closely intertwined in our little corner of the Bible Belt. Responsible citizens of Stokes County, North Carolina, were Bible-believing brethren who went to church every Sunday. The political leaders among us said as much in stump speeches and to the reporter from the *King Times News*. No one was ever going to get elected without the Baptists or the Methodists on their side. But I heard something different in the way those political types talked on the porch at church, smoking cigarettes and shaking hands as we filed out past the preacher and headed to our cars. They didn't talk about the sermon. They didn't even talk about things the preacher seemed to think important—things like salvation, eternal life, and getting born again.

Responsible Christian citizens seemed to talk about real life. Their conversations on the church porch and at the corner store were about the things people spent most of their time doing: going to school, priming tobacco, making money, buying stuff. They talked about farm subsidies and plans to build a new school on the western side of the county. They talked about the economy and the Gulf War. They had their feet on the ground, these patriarchs of our community. And I looked up to them. However high I might soar into the upper echelons of national politics, I knew by instinct that I would have to be like those men: a responsible custodian of the things that really matter down home.

In an old journal, I have a list I wrote at fifteen of "50 Things I Want to Do Before I Die." The list includes things like "Go skydiving" and "Visit every continent." But number one on the list is "Serve as president of the United States." I remember writing that. I remember thinking, *Isn't it a little silly to write that down where someone might read it?* And I remember quoting to myself a verse that I had memorized in Vacation Bible School: "I can do all things through Christ Jesus which strengtheneth me" (Philippians 4:13, KJV). If God wanted a kid from King to grow up and run things His way, then He could make it happen. I knew it as surely as I knew my name.

That certainty gave me the courage to write beyond the confessions of my journal. I wrote to the superintendent of the school system and told him that I thought he should have a student on the school board, and might he consider me? I wrote Senator Jesse Helms and asked how I could get an appointment to serve as a page on Capitol Hill. I wrote bills for the North Carolina youth legislature that the YMCA sponsored. And then I wrote my state representatives to ask if they would take my bills to the real state legislature.

I was delighted to find that these people I had only read about in the newspaper responded to my letters (I didn't know then that it was usually a secretary in their office writing back). Dr. Sells invited me to take a non-voting seat on the Stokes County School Board. Senator Helms referred me to his senior colleague from South Carolina, Senator Strom Thurmond, who said I could come to Washington and work as a page in his office (where I would learn how to use the little machine that put the senator's signature on the bottom of letters he didn't write). The YMCA gave my best friend, Marty, and me the "Best Bill" award for the state of North Carolina when we proposed that punitive damage windfalls be paid to the state for education funding instead of to individuals who had already received retribution. I liked trying to figure this stuff out. Even more, I started to believe that I had been gifted for this sort of work. God was calling me into politics.

Then I met Reverend Barber. It happened in a dimly lit Holiday Inn banquet room just outside Raleigh, the state capital. Marty and I had spent all day listening to young and energetic seminar leaders who were supposed to help us become politically savvy. We were high school participants in a program that the governor's office sponsored for youth with political aspirations. I was one such young Republican, complete with a hand-me-down blue blazer and maroon power tie. Marty was good enough of a friend that he listened to my ideas about saving the soul of America and came along for the ride to Raleigh. His parents were Democrats, but we didn't know enough to think that mattered much.

What we knew was that we were Christians. Marty's dad was our pastor at the Quaker Gap Baptist Church, and we were friends in Christ, born-again brothers who knew in our hearts that God had a plan for our lives. When Reverend Barber stepped to the podium that evening at the Holiday Inn, we recognized his language. He was a preacher. He spoke the language of Scripture, even among young political hopefuls and their secular advisors from the governor's office. That way of speaking had been conspicuously absent from our weekend of reflection on political responsibility and the means of social reform in a democratic society. But Reverend Barber quoted Scripture from memory without citing chapter and verse. Even when he wasn't quoting the Bible, his phrasing echoed the King James English of the Authorized Version. I heard a voice that sounded familiar, and I started to listen.

I remember the slow rhythm of his deep baritone, first thanking his hosts with a plodding intentionality, then announcing his subject for the evening. Reverend Barber was not in a hurry. He was obviously not concerned with the economy of speech that characterizes the public discourse of most politicians. He almost seemed to be stalling. But every once in a while he looked up with a wry smile that gave me the feeling he and I were in on some grand conspiracy together. Whatever it was, I wanted to be part of it.

By the time he started quoting the ABCs of life that his grandmother had taught him, Reverend Barber was beginning to pick up the pace. For each letter, he offered a maxim to guide us on our way. These bits of wisdom, true as they were, didn't open new worlds of insight. I had heard most of them before. But I had never heard them preached with such intensity, as if our very lives depended on them. By the time he got to the letter Z, Reverend Barber was roaring.

Then he told a story. It wasn't a gospel story but rather a stock piece from the annals of motivational speeches — the sort of thing you might read in *Chicken Soup for the Soul.* "I recently read how scientists have observed that the weight of a bumblebee, when compared with the size of its wings, should keep it from ever flying." Reverend Barber paused. He explained the principles of aerodynamics and the difficulty that the anatomy of the bumblebee presents. "Nevertheless, the bumblebee flies. The key to its success," he said with a finger lifted in the air, "is that it keeps flapping those wings." The first time he said it, I heard him. Then he said it again. Only this time, he didn't just say it; he performed it. I watched as this broad-shouldered bear of a man flapped his arms to the beat of his own speech. "Oh the bumblebee — yes, the bumblebee — keeps on flappin' those wings."

Before I knew what was happening to me, I was on my feet, flapping my own arms up and down. I looked around the room to see a couple hundred middle-class white kids in sport coats and business dresses flapping their arms too. Were these the same people I sat around with all morning and afternoon discussing cultural diversity, affirmative action, civic responsibility, and the hopes of democracy? Something had happened to us, almost in an instant. I knew I couldn't explain it, except to say that I felt like flying. I felt free. Maybe for the first time in my life, I felt what Granny could only say in song: "When I die, hallelujah by and by, I'll fly away."

But what did this feeling have to do with "when I die"? It didn't seem like anything died when I stood up to flap my arms along with a couple hundred excitable teenagers. Life went on as usual. The next morning I may well have written the whole thing off as an unmeasured expression of emotionalism. I don't remember. I don't remember now just what I thought about the experience then. Recalling that scene some ten years later, though, I am captivated by its significance. Reverend Barber was the first black Christian I'd ever heard preach. In the dim light of that hotel ballroom, he opened my eyes to the existence of a black church in America. I suppose I knew by then that black Christians existed—and that they worshipped somewhere. I'd heard gospel choirs before. I'd seen the movie *Sister Act*. If I'd thought about it, I probably could have imitated the stereotypical black preacher, quoting lines from Jesse Jackson or Martin Luther King. But I had never thought about it. A white Southern Baptist kid, saturated with Scripture, I'd never thought to ask why everyone in my church looked like me. I'd never reflected on what that might mean for my relationship with other Christians or my relationship with God. I'd never once had to think about it.

Baptist churches in North Carolina were not always segregated. The revival preachers who blazed across the landscape of the South in the last quarter of the eighteenth century were no respecters of persons. They preached Jesus to black and white, slave and free. The good news of salvation was for whoever believeth in his heart, and it was available to the masses. As the Spirit moved, the words of Scripture came to life: "As many of you as have been baptized into Christ have put on Christ. There is neither Jew nor Greek, there is neither bond nor free, there is neither male nor female: for ye are all one in Christ Jesus" (Galatians 3:27-28, KJV). In 1789 the General Committee of Virginia Baptists, just across the border from my home in North Carolina, spoke with a single voice to declare slavery a "violent deprivation of the rights of nature."[1] Many Baptist leaders throughout the South independently freed their slaves. But soon the revival was over, the camp meetings left town, and white folks went to church to find their slaves sitting beside them in the same pews (or in pews very much like theirs in the balcony overhead). They sang the same songs. They prayed the same prayers. They were brothers and sisters in the same body of Christ. The gospel that had been preached with such fervor following the Revolutionary War threatened to revolutionize the social order of the South.

"Consider the moral predicament of the master who sat in church with his slaves," writes fellow Southern Baptist Wendell Berry in his book *The Hidden Wound*. "How could he presume to own the body of a man whose soul he considered as worthy of salvation as his own? To keep this question from articulating itself in his thoughts and demanding an answer, he had to perfect an empty space in his mind, a silence, between heavenly concerns and earthly concerns, between body and spirit." [2] With that division in the mind, a separation of bodies was inevitable. The necessary silence was easier to maintain in congregations where there were no black voices to "talk back." The Bible could be read, the gospel proclaimed, and the God of heaven and spirit worshipped much more easily in the absence of black bodies. Whites eventually forced the retreat of black Christians from the white-dominated churches into black churches of their own.

So the "black church" was born, and along with it a "white church," marked not only by the absence of black Christians but also by the mental division between heaven and earth, faith and politics. This dichotomy, so deeply rooted in our way of being church, did more than lead to racial segregation some two hundred years earlier. It persisted as a block in our imagination, making it impossible to even ask what the church has to do with racial justice, precisely because racial justice was not spiritual but political. Racial justice and integration weren't supposed to have anything to do with our worship on Sunday mornings. Whether they were right or wrong, they just weren't the sort of thing you heard the preacher talk about. Political conversation was reserved for the church's front porch and the corner store. Sure, good Christian citizens had a responsibility to talk about these things, but that had much more to do with being good citizens than with living the gospel as good Christians. So it was that I had felt the need to move from Sunday school piety to front-porch responsibility. And so it was that I had lived some sixteen years in a world saturated with Scripture and drenched in Jesus without ever having to think about the absence of black Christians in my life.

That is, until Reverend Barber stopped by a little gathering of young political hopefuls to give a pep talk and decided to preach. When he did, a new world opened before me about which I knew next to nothing (I didn't even know enough to recognize it as a different world). I certainly didn't imagine then that it was a world I would learn to call home.

Reverend Barber's presence was just so appealing — so wonderfully compelling — that I never stopped to think about what might have to die for me to enter into the world from which he spoke. It didn't occur to me, a kid still trying to navigate the white side of a divided church, that Reverend Barber was introducing me to a whole new way of seeing when he assumed that the gospel is itself political and bodily, that the best thing to do when invited to a governor's conference is to preach. I thought he had sparked an insight — an "aha" moment, like those I'd had when reading a good book or listening to a brilliant teacher. "Reason's wingspan sometimes can be short," the poet Dante wrote.[3] We do not always move from one lesson to the next in logical progression. Sometimes it takes a special grace to lift us to the next step in a line of reasoning. I thought Reverend Barber had come to give me such a boost in my well-ordered ascent toward a responsible Christian politics. I didn't know that the gospel he preached threatened to turn reason on its head. I didn't know that he spoke from another world—a world I would have to die to enter into.

I never stopped to analyze the urge that welled up within me that evening at the Holiday Inn. When Reverend Barber preached, I wanted to fly away, so I stood up and started flapping my arms. My feet didn't leave the ground that evening, but a few weeks later Marty and I were on the road by seven o'clock on a Sunday morning, headed for the Greenleaf Christian Church in Goldsboro, North Carolina, to hear the Reverend William Barber preach again. I didn't know then where that road would take me. All I knew was that I had to fly away.

TWO

If It Had Not Been for the Lord

At the door of the Greenleaf Christian Church, Marty and I met a woman dressed in all white who greeted us warmly, gave us each a program, and invited us to have a seat in the sanctuary. Her uniform was glowing white, stiffly starched and neatly pressed with a crease on the sleeves. It had obviously been carefully cared for, like a soldier's dress coat or a bride's wedding gown. Though clearly functional (it was a uniform, after all), the woman's outfit was formal. She was dressed for a special occasion, and she was inviting us to come in and be a part of it.

I'll confess: I did more observing than worshipping my first Sunday in a black church. The Scriptures were not strange to my ears, nor were the words of the songs foreign to my tongue, but everything seemed new. The dress code was different, the rhythms strange. The aromas were sweet but peculiar to my nose. I'd never smelled those perfumes. I stood when they stood and clapped when they clapped—or tried to. But I knew I wasn't doing what those folks were doing. Though I was trying to be a participant observer, I was an outsider. I had stepped into a strange new world.

A couple of years before my first visit to Greenleaf, I had gone to Europe on a cultural exchange trip with a group from my high school. My mom, who is always eager to learn, came along as a chaperone. (I now suspect she probably wanted to keep an eye on me too.) We saw the great cathedrals of France, stopped for a picture of the tower in Pisa, spent a night in Florence, and continued on to Rome. Sometime when we were in Italy, Mom noticed our bus driver's shoes and, not knowing any Italian, attempted to give him a compliment by making an "okay" sign with her fingers. Unfortunately, that way of making a circle by touching your index finger to your thumb doesn't mean "okay" in Italy. The bus driver was insulted, and our tour guide had to explain the confusion.

So I had learned firsthand that actions don't always mean the same thing in different contexts. What would have been a friendly gesture back home in North Carolina was an insult on a bus in Italy. The difference in perception had everything to do with culture—that thing I had gone to Europe to learn about. People in a different place have a different history, different practices, different ways of thinking about the world. This much I knew. But how was it that people in Goldsboro, North Carolina—people who had lived their whole lives just down the highway from where I grew up—also seemed to have a different culture? How could they do all the same things we did on Sunday morning (and on into the afternoon) and yet seem to do them so differently? Worship itself seemed to mean something different at Greenleaf.

In the Southern Baptist church where I was raised, we had no creed but the Bible, and we observed the liturgy of our Methodist neighbors with some suspicion. (How could anyone really believe prayers they read out of a book?) Worship couldn't be scripted, we thought. Real worship came from the heart. But that's not to say that our worship didn't follow an order. I could recite our unwritten liturgy in my sleep. It was a simple service of songs, prayer, children's sermon, offering, choir special, and sermon. The songs were out of *The Baptist Hymnal*, a collection of 666 revivalist hymns, of which we only ever sang about three dozen. Mom, the choir director, usually led us in verses one, two, and four for no particular reason (as far as I know) except that there were people in the church who couldn't bear the thought of actually having to sing all four verses. The prayers were intoned by men — usually the deacon of the week — who always began by saying, "Our most kind and gracious heavenly Father, we give you thanks . . ." We thanked God for all the ways in which He had made our lives more or less comfortable and, most of all, for the gift of His beloved Son Jesus Christ who died on the cross to forgive us for our sins. We asked for God's blessings. We remembered the sick. And we begged God, if there were anyone in the church that morning who did not already know Jesus Christ as his personal Lord and Savior that he would this very hour invite Jesus into his heart and be saved. Inevitably, people had the opportunity to receive the gift of salvation as the preacher gave his altar call after a twenty-minute sermon. (During revival, a series of evangelistic evening services that we had once a year, you might hear a thirty-minute sermon, with a particularly impassioned altar call. On Sunday mornings, though, the preacher knew to keep it to twenty. There were Crock-Pots and NASCAR races at home waiting for attention.) Somehow every sermon was crafted to show us our need for salvation and to invite us into the joy of eternal life with Christ—which was, of course, the whole point of coming to church. The high point of the liturgy was the sermon. And a sermon ended well if it persuaded someone to return to Jesus—or, even better, to invite Jesus into his or her heart for the first time.

Maybe it was because I had internalized this unwritten liturgy or because we had come especially to hear Reverend Barber in his element, but after more than an hour of singing and clapping and swaying and praising at Greenleaf Christian Church, I began to wonder when we were going to get to the sermon—the main event, so to speak. Some of the songs we sang that morning didn't have more than one simple verse, but the congregation kept repeating that verse over and over again, taking the tune up a key each time around for some songs. After the offering had been gathered, I knew we were approaching the climax. I looked in the bulletin and saw only "Choir Special" left before the sermon. We were getting close, so I settled in to listen to one more song.

I don't remember what song the choir sang that morning, but I do recall that it was received with a great deal of enthusiasm. By the time they got to the first chorus, someone in the congregation was shouting, "Sing choir!" and others were standing on their feet, swaying left and right with each measure and clapping on two and four. After a rousing climax to the song there was a dramatic conclusion and then the musicians picked up the tune again, repeating the chorus once more for a grand finale. By then everyone was on their feet, clapping and saying, "Thank you, Jesus" and "Yes, Lord" (at Greenleaf, "Lord" was pronounced with three syllables: "Law-uh-duh").

In the midst of this celebration, a woman in the choir loft began shouting louder than everyone else. She threw her hands in the air and stomped her feet on the floor of the choir loft, sending a deep boom through the noisy room each time. Then she began to scream, almost as if she were in pain, except that between her screams she was thanking Jesus and praising God. Tears streamed down her face. Her choir robe swung back and forth as she stomped her feet. She moved faster and faster, shouting louder and louder, until all of a sudden she threw up her hands and fell to the floor.

I looked over to Marty, concerned this woman might have had a heart attack in the middle of the worship service but not knowing what to do. Marty seemed equally confused. Ushers, like the woman dressed in white whom we had met at the door, gathered around the woman and were fanning her with the pieces of card stock on wooden paint stirrers that were beside the hymnals in the back of each pew and bore advertisements for the local funeral home. If singing a choir special could send you to the grave, no wonder the undertakers advertised in church. But after a few minutes of fanning, the woman in the choir loft stood up with some help from the ushers and walked out the side door of the choir loft. All the while the music kept playing, most of the choir kept swaying, and the saints at Greenleaf kept praising the Lord.

I later learned that what Marty and I witnessed that Sunday is called "falling out." It doesn't necessarily happen every week, but in the black church tradition it's an experience common enough to have a name. When someone gets so excited by the experience of worship that they dance and shout until they fall to the floor, you call it falling out. I'd never heard of or seen anything like it in the Southern Baptist churches where I grew up. What was it about worship at Greenleaf that could leave someone lying flat on the floor? And why was an experience like that unimaginable back at home? At sixteen I could hardly articulate the questions, but I carried them with me as Marty and I drove back to King, our stomachs full of the fried chicken and biscuits we had been served after worship at Greenleaf. I carried the questions with me as I returned to another world.

"The enslavement of an estimated ten million Africans over a period of almost four centuries in the Atlantic slave trade was a tragedy of such scope that it is difficult to imagine, much less comprehend," writes historian Albert J. Raboteau at the beginning of his classic work *Slave Religion*.[1] People whose lives had been deeply rooted in the stories and practices of family, tribe, and land in Africa were suddenly and without explanation torn from their past and packed into ships that carried them across an ocean and into another world. It was, needless to say, a world they did not choose. This new world of American slavery was marked not only by displacement but also by separation from clan and kin. Black bodies were packed indiscriminately into slave ships for the long Middle Passage, during which those who did not survive were simply cast overboard, covering the sea floor with as many bodies as made it to the other side. Everyone who made that journey across the Atlantic watched someone beside them die. Those who survived were taken immediately from the ships to an auction block, where their bodies were assessed as property and then sold to white men. They became a people who, in the eyes of America's new economy, were owned. As property, black slaves in America were put to work at the will of their masters, beaten and sometimes killed when their performance was deemed unsatisfactory. Parents and children were sold and separated as the white master's economic considerations required. Black women were raped while their husbands stood by, unable to defend those they loved against white men who insisted that they were exercising an economic right. This was the reality of the New World for people with black skin. Raboteau is right: It is a history that is difficult to even imagine.

Add to this history, however, the fact that the very same white men who bought black bodies, beat black bodies, and forced themselves upon black bodies also saw to it that the good news of Jesus Christ was preached to black souls. Granted, the evangelization of slaves was not always a high priority for white masters and was sometimes even avoided for fear that it would plant a seed of rebellion in the slave's spirit. Nevertheless, black folk in America learned the gospel story from the same people who held them in slavery. The miracle of the black church in America is that somehow, in a story told by oppressors, the oppressed heard good news—and believed it. Grasping hold of a personal relationship with the God whom their masters claimed to worship, slaves were able to distinguish between the liberating truth of Christ's message and the white man's abuse of Holy Scripture for his own purposes. No one articulated this distinction more clearly than the ex-slave and abolitionist Frederick Douglass:

> Between the Christianity of this land, and the Christianity of Christ, I recognize the widest, possible difference—so wide, that to receive the one as good, pure, and holy, is of necessity to reject the other as bad, corrupt, and wicked. To be the friend of the one is of necessity to be the enemy of the other. I love the pure, peaceable, and impartial Christianity of Christ: I therefore hate the corrupt, slave-holding, women-whipping, cradle-plundering, partial and hypocritical Christianity of this land. Indeed, I can see no reason but the most deceitful one for calling the religion of this land Christianity.[2]

Douglass's "Christianity of Christ" was a message that somehow spoke all the more powerfully for having been taken right out of the white master's mouth. This God, who said to his people, "Thou shalt not steal," stood in judgment over the white master who had stolen black bodies from Africa and forced them to work for his financial gain. Just as the God of Israel had defeated Pharaoh in Egypt, black slaves believed the Lord could send another Moses to lead them out of bondage and into Canaan Land. Indeed, when freedom from slavery finally did come after centuries of suffering on American soil, black Christians praised the God of Israel who had brought them freedom in Christ and made liberty real on the ground of history in the Emancipation Proclamation of 1863. The stories of Israel and Jesus were fused beautifully in the spirituals that are our best record of the theology of slave religion.

O Mary don't you weep (don't you mourn)
O Mary don't you weep (don't you mourn)
Pharaoh's army got drowned
O Mary don't you weep.

Sorrow was turned to joy by this God of Israel, made into a man in Jesus Christ. "If it had not been for the Lord on my side," the old saints asked, "tell me, where would I be? O tell me, where would I be?"

Some scholars of Afro-American religion have argued that traditions of hand clapping, dance, and "spirit possession" in the black church tradition are simply remnants of African religious traditions that were preserved in the slave communities of America. "Falling out," according to these scholars, could be understood as an African cultural expression modified for Christian worship and passed down through the centuries to that woman in the choir at Greenleaf Christian Church. In this way of thinking, the differences in worship style between black and white churches are simply the result of two cultures. The problem with this interpretation is that it doesn't take into account the experience of black people in America during those centuries in which some parts of their African heritage may or may not have been passed down. Nor does it account for the memory of suffering that inevitably shapes the worship of black Christians. But most importantly, it does not take seriously enough the overwhelming grace of God that the black Christian celebrates in her worship. "Lord! Lord!" exclaimed Minnie Fulkes, a former slave, "I hope yo' young fo'ks will never know what slavery is, an' will never suffer as yo' foreparents. O God! God! I'm livin' to tel' de tale to yo', honey. Yes, Jesus, yo've spared me."[3]

Minnie Fulkes, like the woman who fell out my first Sunday at Reverend Barber's church, worshipped God out of a particular history. She understood herself to be part of a people who could not take their existence for granted. If it had not been for the Lord on her side, Minnie Fulkes might well have died at the hands of her white master. And if it had not been for the Lord on her side, the woman in the choir at Greenleaf might well have never been born. But the fact of the matter was that she had been born—and born again—despite the wiles of the Devil and the will of white supremacy. By the grace of God, she had lived to sing a song of praise to her God one Sunday morning in Goldsboro, North Carolina. And that was something worth getting excited about—so excited, in fact, that she passed out. Such overwhelming excitement is not peculiar to black folks. I've seen it on commercials when the Publisher's Clearing House delivers a ten-million-dollar check to a poor white woman. Historians tell us that it was not uncommon among white folks at the revivals of the eighteenth century in America, nor would it be unheard of in multiethnic Pentecostal churches today. More than just a culturally conditioned experience, falling out seems to have something to do with being overwhelmed by the goodness of God. After the experience of oppression and suffering in a world that she didn't choose, a choir member at Greenleaf could be knocked down by the goodness of Jesus. The intensity of her worship had opened for me a window into her world.

Not long after that first trip to visit Greenleaf, Marty called Reverend Barber and invited him to come and preach the baccalaureate service at our high school the next spring. We didn't think much of it. It just seemed like a good opportunity to introduce people in King to our new friend from Goldsboro. Marty was graduating that year and told the planning committee that he knew just the preacher for this event. Since he was himself the son of a preacher, I guess the committee figured that he knew what he was talking about. Without any questions, William Barber was scheduled to address the graduating class of South Stokes High School.

When I was a student there, South Stokes was a county school between two towns: King and Walnut Cove. I don't remember knowing anyone from Walnut Cove before going to high school. When I started the ninth grade, I looked around my classrooms and the basketball court and noticed that nearly half of the new faces were black. Only two black guys — Norman and Lee — had come with us from Chestnut Grove Junior High School in King. The other black faces were from Walnut Cove. On a campus that sat in the middle of an old cow field between two Southern towns, public education had brought white and black together.

On the afternoon of the baccalaureate service, Marty and

I met the Barber family minivan in the school parking lot. We greeted Reverend Barber with hugs, and he introduced us to his brother-in-law, whom he had brought along for support. Though he had traveled quite a bit in North Carolina, this was Reverend Barber's first time in Stokes County. Black folks knew about Stokes County, he said with raised eyebrows. He'd heard stories about how this used to be "Klan country." It had never occurred to me that it might be frightening for someone with black skin to visit my hometown, but Reverend Barber had been afraid to come to Stokes County alone. My world looked different through his eyes.

It wasn't until after I had left King for college that I read in a book what black folks from Walnut Cove had to say about King. One black man told Henry Wiencek, who was researching the Hairston family, that King was "as bad as Mississippi or Alabama — you wouldn't want to get caught there after dark." He recalled graffiti on a road sign outside King saying, "Niggers — keep on thru."[4] When I asked some of my family about the sign, they said they remembered seeing it as late as the mid-1980s. This was the world I grew up in.

But until that day in the spring of 1998 when Reverend Barber came to preach at South Stokes, I had never imagined Stokes County as a dangerous place. Backward, provincial, even boring — yes. All these things I had thought. But dangerous? How could my home be dangerous? Stokes County was farm country, populated by good and simple folk — folk who were my people. How could my people be the enemy?

By the time I studied North Carolina history in King's public schools, the Ku Klux Klan was a part of the past that we read about in textbooks. Not only was it history, but I got the sense that the KKK was someone else's history. In my mind the Klan belonged to the Deep South of Alabama, which had resisted integration and civil rights to the embarrassment of all Southerners. But George Wallace and Bull Connor were older than my grandparents. My mom had conscientiously taught us Hartgrove boys a New South color-blindness, which she never tired of reinforcing with a story about how proud she was the day my older brother Josh got mad at a black kid on the playground and came to her to tell on him. (I've never been sure in this story where the playground was with black children playing on it.) "When I asked him which child he was talking about," Mom would always say with obvious delight, "he pointed to the little black boy and said, 'That one in the red shirt.'" Josh called him not by the color of his skin but by the color of his shirt. My mom's sons were raised not to see color.

As a teenager, though, I learned from Reverend Barber that I was white. I had, of course, known this before—had known it as a fact, like any other bit of data. I knew when filling out a personal information form at the doctor's office that my hair was brown, my eyes hazel, and my skin white. But "white" was just that: the color of my skin (though I remember on one occasion writing "tan" in the blank beside "race" because it seemed to me a more accurate description). I did not imagine that "white" said anything about who I was or that it in any way connected me to other people with white skin. I'd certainly never thought that it tied me to those ignorant men of another era who ran around in bedsheets. But Reverend Barber had heard that Stokes County was Klan country once upon a time. And he had brought his brother-in-law along as a hedge against history when he came to preach at my high school.

The baccalaureate sermon was well received, and we had a good time afterward, eating dinner with Reverend Barber and his brother-in-law at Marty's parents' house. After Reverend Barber had gone back to Goldsboro, though, I couldn't help but look around at King and wonder when it had stopped being Klan country. A man about my dad's age who would have graduated from South Stokes in the mid-1970s told me a story about how as a teenager he had returned home late one night from a date just down Highway 52 in Rural Hall to find a Klan rally blocking the street and the adjacent parking lot of a drive-in movie theater, only a mile or so from his house. Disturbed by the scene and not wanting to stop for conversation, he pointed the hood of his Mustang at the crowd in the street and stepped on the gas. They jumped out of the way, and he passed through without stopping. Some two decades later, he recalled the scene as a strange and distant memory.

Twenty years, though, is not really so long, I thought, as I listened to him. Most of the faces beneath those hoods were probably still around today, even if slightly more wrinkled. I scanned the crowd at church on Sunday morning and wondered if any of those men had ever donned a robe out on old Highway 52. If so, how did they remember those nights? Had their minds changed? Or had their robes just become unfashionable? No one ever talked about it, and I knew enough at seventeen to know I shouldn't ask.

But I've carried the questions with me. In the summer of 2005, a Truth and Reconciliation Commission was convened in Greensboro, North Carolina, about forty miles from King, to hear testimony about a massacre that occurred there on November 3, 1979, when neo-Nazis and members of the Ku Klux Klan showed up at a "Death to the Klan" rally and opened fire. Thirteen protestors were hit. Five died from the wounds they suffered that day. The Klansmen, however, were acquitted by an all-white jury in their criminal trial. Despite accusations that they were stirring up old trouble that was better left alone, the Commission invited people from all sides of the tragic event to come forward and offer testimony to the community about what happened on November 3, 1979. One of the men who came forward was Virgil Griffin, Imperial Wizard of the Cleveland Knights of the Ku Klux Klan.

I drove over to Greensboro to hear Mr. Griffin's testimony because, more than anything, I wanted to see and hear a real-live North Carolina Klansman. Part of me wanted to see if he looked anything like those men from my home church. He was not ashamed of the Klan, he testified, and he thought he had just as much a right to be part of it as a black man did to join the NAACP. He didn't hate blacks, but he believed that the Bible spoke against "race-mixin'." Mr. Griffin's testimony about the events of November 3, 1979, was vague and somewhat evasive, I thought. He did say he would have never gone that day if he had known what was going to happen. But I was most interested in his answers to a series of questions from one of the commissioners about the role of the Klan in North Carolina:

"Mr. Griffin, are you presently a member of the Ku Klux Klan?" the commissioner asked.

"Yes, I am. Will be until I die. I'm the Imperial Wizard of the Cleveland Knights of the Ku Klux Klan. I'm over several states."

To clarify, the commissioner asked, "And is that, you said, the Cleveland Knights of the Ku Klux Klan?"

"Yes," Mr. Griffin nodded with his jaw set.

"And is that group still active?"

"Yeah, we're active."

"Can you say how many members are part of that group?"

Virgil Griffin laughed. "No, I can't tell you how many members we have."

"Okay. Can you say what kinds of activities the group is involved in today?"

"Well, uh, we're trying to bring prayer back into the schools, mainly—and get drugs and weapons out. And, uh, we help people. We do things for the community."[5] He said it with a hint of defeat in his voice. But I also heard in Mr. Griffin's voice the embattled conviction of simple and faithful men from my home church—men whom I've always respected. Whether any of them ever wore the hood, I knew they had inherited the world Mr. Griffin was trying to defend. We all had, whether we knew it or not.

The summer after Reverend Barber came to King, our Southern Baptist Convention (SBC) held its annual meeting in Salt Lake City, Utah, where they voted to add a statement to the Baptist Faith and Message which said a woman should "submit herself graciously" to her husband's leadership. The Convention's newly elected president told reporters that the statement was our response to a "time of growing crisis in the family." But my family thought it a strange response. In our home Mom clearly had leadership gifts in her own right, and Dad had always been glad to acknowledge that. He did not send down decrees to us as a family. As a matter of fact, he often deferred to Mom's wisdom about family decisions. At the very least, the two of them usually had a good argument about things they disagreed on.

And though Dad was a deacon at our church, he was also a student in Mom's Sunday school class, where she led men and women in the study of God's Holy Word. Why, then, did our church's convention need to tell her to "graciously submit"? I recall someone noting that Ephesians 5:21 said, "Submit to one another out of reverence for Christ." But that was meant for all Christians. Why wasn't anyone proposing a statement that men also submit to their wives—or to their mothers?

I remember being aware that summer for the first time in

my life of people outside the church talking about us Southern Baptists. There were articles in the newspaper. Pastors were interviewed on the evening news. One night a professor from Wake Forest University was on the local evening news talking about the history of Southern Baptists. He said he thought it was important to note that Southern Baptists have always been concerned about how to read the passages on submission from the end of the book of Ephesians. The SBC was founded in 1845 because slave-holding Baptists in the South insisted that Ephesians 6:5 — "Slaves, obey your earthly masters" — was biblical justification for the institution of chattel slavery. Of course, none of us believed that anymore by the end of the twentieth century. But I was struck by the thought that our history of justifying slavery was somehow still with us in this debate about submission. Being white in Klan country wasn't just about what some of the old guys at our church may or may not have done twenty years ago. I realized that summer that it also affected the way we read Scripture. And Scripture, I knew, was at the very heart of our world. Whiteness, it seemed, colored everything.

The justification and defense of slavery among Southern Baptists and other white Christians in North Carolina did not come without a heightened sense of responsibility for the souls of those dark bodies my forebears had enslaved. In December of 1859, just before the outbreak of America's Civil War, the *North Carolina Christian Advocate*, a Methodist paper, claimed that "everybody who believes in religion at all admits that it is the duty of Christians to give religious instruction to the slave population of the Southern States. To deny the safety and propriety of preaching the gospel to the Negroes is either to abandon Christianity or to admit that slavery is condemned by it."[6] A Southern Baptist couldn't have said it better. At seventeen I knew that the SBC had the largest mission board of any denomination in America. I had myself already traveled with mission teams to Zimbabwe and Venezuela. But I had never imagined any connection between our missionary fervor and our history of justifying and defending slavery.

Having seen my world anew through Reverend Barber's eyes, I began to notice things that had been hidden in plain sight. White Christians whose identity as Southern Baptists had been defined by a split from Northern Baptists over slavery had soothed their pangs of conscience about owning fellow human beings by convincing themselves that the slaves really were better off if their souls were saved while their bodies were in bondage than if body and soul had perished together in Africa. The Civil War had brought an end to slavery in America, but not to the white Christian worldview that was constructed around slavery as a given. A sense of responsibility for the salvation of heathen souls had compelled Southern Baptist missionaries to go forth for generations proclaiming white salvation to the dark masses of Africa and South America. That I had already traveled with mission teams to both of those continents by the age of seventeen just made me a good Southern Baptist.

But this drive to export our gospel to all nations had not only produced missionaries to foreign lands. At home our high calling had also required defenders of our way of life to fight the good fight on native soil. Most recently that meant insisting on wifely submission during a "time of growing crisis in the family." But as Virgil Griffin of the KKK would later make clear to me, defense of family and community was what the Klan had understood itself to be doing all along. Their mission was tied to what we did together at church every Sunday morning and Wednesday evening and at the occasional potluck supper in between. With or without the bedsheets, I was a citizen of Klan country. And my love for Reverend Barber didn't change that one bit.

In his book *Jesus and the Disinherited*, the great black preacher Howard Thurman wrote,

> The masses of men live with their backs constantly against the wall. They are the poor, the disinherited, the dispossessed. What does our religion say to them? The issue is not what it counsels them to do for others . . . but what religion offers to meet their own needs. The search for an answer to this question is perhaps the most important religious quest of modern life.[7]

The white gospel I learned as a child in the Southern Baptist church had convicted me as a teenager to ask what I could do for others. "To whom much is given, much will be required," the Bible says (see Luke 12:48). I wanted to give my very best for the sake of those less fortunate—for the sake of dark peoples in the uttermost parts of the earth who had never had the chance to ask Jesus into their hearts. But all the time there was a brokenness so deep within me and my people's history that I needed someone else to show it to me. Of course, Reverend Barber could see it the moment he first looked at me. To his eyes my history was written on my skin. And mine was a history of sin. But the answer to what religion might offer my deep need—that "most important religious question of modern life"—was yet a mystery to me. Religion, it seemed, was much of the problem.

But I did not leave the church in search of answers. I did not leave, I think, because the one who had shown me my deep need was also a preacher of the gospel to the disinherited. Reverend Barber was heir to a vision for God's kingdom that had given hope to generations of slaves who suffered at the hands of my people. But in Reverend Barber's vision of God's beloved community, it wasn't just white folks who were "my people." Because he and I had both been baptized in Jesus' name, Reverend Barber was my brother—an elder brother who was himself on a "most important religious quest." The crossing of our paths had meant for me the discovery of two worlds—one black, one white—neither of which I had been able to see before, despite the fact that I had lived my whole life in the latter. But those worlds and their realities were sustained by the everyday practices of particular communities—communities like King and Greenleaf. That Marty and I had visited Greenleaf Christian Church meant a door had been opened for Reverend Barber to come to King. That King had met Reverend Barber meant other points of contact between two worlds—connections I could not have imagined. But, of course, none of this was about what I could imagine. It was, instead, the beginning of a quest toward the God who knows our every care and supplies our every need. Saints who know that God learn to sing, "If it had not been for the Lord on my side, tell me, where would I be? O tell me, where would I be?"

THREE

I Need You, You Need Me

I never left the church universal, but I did leave King—and with it, my home church—not long after Reverend Barber opened my eyes to the racialized reality I had grown up in. I left because I was restless, because I had a head full of questions that I didn't think King could help me answer. I left because leaving seemed exciting to my teenage soul, aching to individuate. And I left, ultimately, because I could. An advertisement printed on heavy-stock glossy paper caught my eye outside the guidance counselor's office at my high school. "STUDY IN GERMANY," it said in bold letters above a description of the United States Congress-Bundestag exchange program that had been initiated after World War II in hopes that Germans and Americans would not kill each other again if students from each country spent a year in the other, learning to appreciate the people and their culture. Because it was a government-sponsored exchange, participants didn't have to pay anything for their year of study abroad. I talked to my parents, filled out an application, and after a couple of interviews received an invitation to finish high school in Germany.

In his classic work *The Souls of Black Folk*, W.E.B. DuBois wrote that the only two times in his life he ever felt free from the shadow of white supremacy were before he was awakened to his blackness as a young boy and when he studied in Germany as a graduate student.[1] When I left King for Germany I had not read DuBois, nor did I really have much of a clue that the stirrings in my soul that were pushing me away from home might have something to do with my growing sense of confusion about being Christian and being white in Stokes County. But I did have some sense — a feeling in my gut — that learning German and studying in Europe would make me cultured. And I had already gathered enough to know that people of culture who read books and went to plays in the big city of Winston-Salem didn't talk about black folks the same way the good ol' boys at the gas station in King did. I had already learned from Mrs. Patsy Ginns, my English teacher, that if you open up the back of your throat and let your tongue bounce off your teeth when you talk, that Southern accent that is so often associated with ignorance will fade away. Even if I didn't know where it came from, I could already feel a pull away from the South and its history of racism to a land of promise, north of the Mason-Dixon line and across the great Atlantic at the bottom of which some fifteen million black bodies lay buried. So I found myself on a 747, high above what DuBois had called the "color line," flying away from Klan country to the enlightened world of culture in Europe.

Meanwhile, what I didn't know was that Reverend Barber's visit to King had affected Marty's dad, our pastor, every bit as much as it had shaken me. Reverend Jim Baldwin was a Presbyterian of good Southern Democrat stock who had turned Southern Baptist in the 1970s when he fell in love with Marty's momma, ENan, and got saved going to the Baptist church with her. A gregarious soul, he had been the pastor of Quaker Gap Baptist Church for over a decade when my family moved our membership there just as I was starting high school. Truth be told, Jim's intellect, wit, and care for me probably had as much to do with my staying in the church as Reverend Barber's witness did. Jim was a preacher who could say something interesting about the Scripture text on Sunday morning, tell a good joke at a family gathering during the week, and beat me silly at Trivial Pursuit on Saturday night. Even though I was already a foot taller than him when we met, I always looked up to Jim, as did most everyone at Quaker Gap. A city boy by birth, Jim had won the hearts of his backwoods brethren by learning to speak the farmers' lingo, admitting ignorance about local custom when it was already clear to all, and even serving as chaplain to the volunteer fire department. The people of Quaker Gap knew that Jim was a pastor they could trust. So no one objected when he announced the fall after I had left for Germany that the Reverend William Barber of Greenleaf Christian Church would be preaching the homecoming service at Quaker Gap.

I listened to Reverend Barber's sermon six days after his visit to King on an audiocassette that my parents mailed me. Before I listened to the sermon, though, I heard reports over the telephone about how the entire Greenleaf choir and their families, some hundred people in all, had come and delighted the congregation with songs. "We've come to add our part to the stew," their choir director had said. Everyone loved it. After the service there was a potluck in the fellowship hall with plenty of casseroles and fried chicken for all. And then everyone went back to the sanctuary for more singing, from both churches' choirs this time. As folks gathered together, Reverend Barber stood on stage, looking around the room, and asked, "Where Pastor Baldwin?" According to one report, Jim stepped up to the platform from behind Reverend Barber and peeped, "Here I is!" The whole place erupted in laughter. In the pulpit of a little Southern Baptist church in Klan country, a black pastor and a white pastor — two brothers in Christ — were having fun with each other. Whatever people at Quaker Gap may have thought of black folks over the years, it was clear that God had made fellowship across the color line possible.

The text for Reverend Barber's sermon was Galatians 3:26-29:

> You are all sons of God through faith in Christ Jesus, for all of you who were baptized into Christ have clothed yourself with Christ. There is neither Jew nor Greek, slave nor free, male nor female, for you are all one in Christ Jesus. If you belong to Christ, then you are Abraham's seed, and heirs according to the promise.

Having heard reports of the wonderful time everyone had at homecoming, I listened as Reverend Barber read the Scripture, considered his context, and soared toward a vision of black and white together in God's kingdom come on earth as it is in heaven. I listened at my desk in a little room on the second floor, over-looking the German village of Wuerselen. I listened with my eyes closed, and I wept.

In Germany I learned a new language and began to be able to articulate the feelings that had driven me away from home and moved me to tears when I listened to Reverend Barber proclaim, "You are all one in Christ Jesus," to a sanctuary filled with black and white faces. Pouring over stacks of books in German and in

English, I learned the great tradition of Enlightenment philosophy. Just after America gained its independence from England, the German philosopher Immanuel Kant wrote that "enlightenment is man's emergence from his self-imposed immaturity."[2] Self-imposed immaturity sounded like a pretty good description of what I was running away from. Racism, it seemed, was a kind of ignorance, an immaturity in the soul of the South. Like any teenager, I was trying to grow up and find my identity as a mature adult. But my psychological need to individuate was complicated by this broader sense of a social immaturity that Reverend Barber had shown me.

My people's accent sounded "backward," I reasoned, because we were indeed behind, underdeveloped, and unenlightened. But if Kant was right—if this immaturity really was self-imposed—then another future was possible. Just as I could fly to Germany, learn a language, and start a new life on my own, so too could Quaker Gap, if given the opportunity, see the light and recognize our need for reconciliation with black brothers and sisters. What we needed was education—an articulate Reverend Barber to show us our need for each other and teach us that God had already made unity possible in the gift of Jesus Christ. If we each added our part to the stew, as Greenleaf's choir director had said, America could become the proverbial melting pot that it claimed to be—a nation in which all the races of the world are blended together for the sake of something greater than any of its constituent parts. Maturity was within reach, my hormones shouted to my seventeen-year-old body. At the same time, I was beginning to learn the Enlightenment logic by which the West has imagined that all people can grow into a civilized world order. Maybe a multicultural society of tolerance and goodwill was also possible.

Before going to Germany I had met with the guidance counselor at South Stokes to plan for college after finishing high school
in Germany. She asked what schools I was interested in, and I said
I had thought about the University of North Carolina at Chapel
Hill, our best state school, and Davidson, the liberal arts college
with Presbyterian roots where Pastor Jim had done his under-
graduate degree. I also told her I had heard a guy named Tony
Campolo give a talk that I really liked at Wake Forest University
in Winston-Salem. I remembered him saying that he taught at
Eastern College, a Christian liberal arts school that intention-
ally integrated faith, reason, and social justice in its curriculum.
"Where is that?" she asked. I told her I thought he had said
Philadelphia. "Well, I'll tell you what," she said. "I'll get you all
the information you need for these in-state schools. We have very
good schools here in North Carolina. If you want to look at out-
of-state schools, you can do that on your own." I decided that day
I would go to Eastern.

So after a brief return to King in the summer of 1999, I
packed up my Chevy Blazer and headed north, past D.C., where
I had flirted with politics a couple of years earlier, to Philadelphia.
I moved my stuff into Hainer Hall and met James, my new roommate from West Philly. All I knew about West Philly was that Will
Smith had sung about getting out of it in the theme song to *The
Fresh Prince of Bel-Air*. Like Smith, James was black. A generation
earlier, his mother had packed her bags and made the same trip
from North Carolina that I had just finished in eight hours flat
on two tanks of gas. She had come north with hopes of a better
future, believing that if she worked hard enough James could get
a good education and have a better life than she had known down
South. For James' momma, that drive north on I-95 had been a
flight to freedom from a way of life in which black women were

treated, as Zora Neale Hurston once said, like the "mule of the earth."[3] I had not suffered as she had, but I was running too. I was chasing after a vision half-born, longing to find a new way of life that would make Reverend Barber's vision a reality. How do black people and white people become one in Christ Jesus? And what does that look like? I went to Eastern College asking those questions and believing that an education worth having would help me answer them.

The German word for education is *Bildung*. It comes from the verb *bilden*, which can be translated into English as "to form" or "to shape." Bildung is education that is also formation in a way of life. This is why Bildung can also be translated as "culture." As it had in Germany, culture continued to play a large part in my education at Eastern. As part of a new program there called the Templeton Honors College, I read books about the "culture wars" and the disintegration of values in American culture. For my whole freshman year I took a course in Great Books of Western Culture. Together with Plato and Aristotle, Dante and Kant, I got to think about life's big questions — who we are, what we're here for, where we're going — and always the more specific question: How do black people and white people become one in Christ Jesus? The urgency of the question was as close to me as my dorm room.

It made no sense to James when I told him I had decided to major in philosophy. What was I going to do with that? James liked to talk about the big questions of life too, but he knew his momma was counting on her son to get an education that he could do something with. James told me the day I met him that he had come to Eastern to major in urban economic development. We talked together about the possibility of a new economic order where the poor would not suffer so that the rich could be rich.

The biblical vision of God's economy had inspired James when he heard it preached in what he called his "hood." He had come to Eastern to get the tools he needed to help build a new economic order in West Philly. James wasn't wasting any time on abstract questions. He had things that he knew God was calling him to do in the world.

I spent some time trying to ground myself in the reality that James knew so well. My first week at Eastern I met Leah Wilson, a fellow freshman from Southern California who told me about a handful of recent graduates from Eastern who had befriended some homeless families in Philly and, after the families got homes, had decided to move into their economically depressed neighborhood. These young Christians lived together as a little community they called "The Simple Way" and said they were trying to live out the part in the book of Acts where it says, "All the believers were one in heart and mind. No one claimed that any of his possessions was his own, but they shared everything they had" (Acts 4:32). When these folks learned that their neighbors didn't have beds to sleep on, they gave them theirs and slept on the floor. They said they had learned from Mother Teresa that "we can do no great things, only small things with great love." So they lived together doing small things: sharing meals with homeless friends, playing with kids in the neighborhood, talking to prostitutes and drug addicts. Leah introduced me to The Simple Way, and I heard their story of downward mobility from the heights of suburban sprawl to the depths of Pennsylvania's poorest district. They were, for the most part, white middle-class college students who had fallen in love with some homeless folks in an abandoned Catholic cathedral and felt as if they had rediscovered the church of the first century. "I want to know Christ," Paul wrote in his letter to the Philippians, "and the power of his resurrection and the fellowship of sharing in his sufferings, becoming like him in his death, and so, somehow, to attain to the resurrection from the dead" (3:10-11). At The Simple Way, I met Christians who had heard Jesus calling them not to flee from the deep suffering of the world but to embrace it, even to the point of death, and so to learn the logic of resurrection. "Unless a kernel of wheat falls to the ground and dies, it remains only a single seed," Jesus said (John 12:24). Leah and I, along with a couple of other friends, started going to the city every chance we got to hang out at The Simple Way with these odd Christians and their homeless friends. Single mothers, men without teeth, and twentysomethings with dreadlocks became our teachers.

Meanwhile, Leah and I were also obliged to attend cultural events in the city with our Honors College. One day we were eating lunch on a park bench with our new homeless friends. The next evening we were being served by black waitresses at Philadelphia's prestigious Union League. I'll never forget the evening one of our professors took us to hear the Philadelphia symphony. We went backstage after the concert to meet the conductor and guest pianist before stepping out into the cold night air to walk to our school vans. Somewhere along the way a few of us in the back of the group struck up a conversation with a homeless man who started walking with us. Eventually, he asked if any of us had some spare change, and one of my classmates gave him a few quarters. At the next stoplight our professor called us all together on a busy street corner, raised his finger in the air, and made a pronouncement for all to hear: "Never, never, never give money to a panhandler!" Then he turned sharply on his heel and proceeded silently to the vans. No conversation. The enlightened professor had made his judgment and sent down his decree.

Leah was so mad that she told me a few days later she thought she needed to drop out of the Honors College. I felt myself torn between two educations. On one hand, I was reading great books, listening to good music, and learning to appreciate good art so that my mind could be formed to know the true, the good, and the beautiful—those things that are ultimate in human life. On the other hand, the Bible and our experience on the streets were calling us to leave the ivory tower and learn from the poor and oppressed what was wrong with the social order and, perhaps, what a better world could look like. I was frustrated and felt stuck. Philosophy had been an incredible gift to me, offering hope that it really was possible to rise above the "self-imposed immaturity" of Klan country to some better future. But my climb into the upper realm of Ideas seemed to take me further and further from the reality of suffering that so many people, most of them black, knew on the streets of Philadelphia. Yet that suffering seemed to open their eyes and mine to the good news of the message Jesus brought to Jewish peasants living under Roman occupation in first-century Palestine. Jesus had taught sharecroppers that the only way up is down into the ground, like the seeds they planted year after year. Which way do you go to find God's kingdom, up or down? I started feeling as though God were calling me to take the low road.

So I pitched the idea to James one night in our room. If Jesus came to preach good news to the poor, emptied Himself, and became a man of no reputation, doesn't that mean we need to follow after Jesus in the way of voluntary poverty? James smiled and shook his head back and forth. "Man, I been poor long enough." I told him about the folks at The Simple Way who had given up their beds. He told me that our room on campus was the first place he had ever had a bed. Back and forth we went, trying to make sense of where we had come from and where God was leading us. I was running from white privilege, discovering God's love for the poor, and trying to figure out how God could possibly love me. James had seen the evils of destitution, knew that God wanted something else for the world, and was struggling to learn how he could work with God to relieve suffering in West Philly.

I began to see that I was romanticizing poverty by looking down at it from my lofty ideals of beauty and truth. It was easy to talk about giving things up and the beauty of simplicity when I had never had to go without. But James knew what it was like to be poor. He knew that God loved the hungry and the homeless. And he also knew that Jesus multiplied the loaves and fishes to feed the hungry and adopted us into God's family so that we could have homes everywhere we go — even now, "in this present age." Jesus didn't ask us to take a vow of poverty, but instead to become part of a family where rich and poor share together so that the rich are no longer rich and the poor are no longer poor. "Give me neither poverty nor riches," Proverbs says, "but give me only my daily bread. Otherwise, I may have too much and disown you and say, 'Who is the LORD?' Or I may become poor and steal, and so dishonor the name of my God" (Proverbs 30:8-9).

The problem with wealth seemed to be that it too easily became a god for both the rich and the poor. But Jesus said, "You cannot serve both God and Money" (Luke 16:13). Choosing to serve God meant becoming part of a family in which I needed James and he needed me. The good gifts of God need to be redistributed among us in a broken world so that everyone can enjoy the life we were made for.

I read these instructions addressed to Timothy as if they had been written for me: "Command those who are rich in this present world not to be arrogant nor to put their hope in wealth, which is so uncertain, but to put their hope in God . . . so that they may take hold of the life that is truly life" (1 Timothy 6:17,19). Reverend Barber had helped me see back in North Carolina both the existence and the uncertainty of white privilege—that I had inherited an unjust way of life and that I could not simply accept it for what it was. But now James was pushing me further, forcing me to admit that I could not simply refuse to climb the social ladder, drop out of school, and claim holiness in a life of poverty. To do so would be to accept the terms of a twisted and broken world. Instead, God was calling me to see that I needed James. I needed James to save me from my romantic ideals and to show me the reality God was inviting us into together. In the context of a living relationship across the color line, somewhere between the ideas of the Great Books and the reality of the streets, we were learning the truth of a song that I would later learn to sing in the black churches of America:

> I need you, you need me.
> We're all a part of God's body.
> Stand with me, agree with me.
> We're all a part of God's body.
> It is his will that every need be supplied.
> You are important to me.
> I need you to survive.

Meanwhile back in North Carolina, Quaker Gap and Greenleaf continued the relationship that had begun when Reverend Barber and a hundred of his parishioners came to King for Quaker Gap's homecoming. Reverend Barber sent an invitation for Jim to come preach in Goldsboro, along with a request that he bring his choir with him. So Quaker Gap sent about a hundred folks down to Goldsboro one Sunday morning and shared in worship with our new sister church. A number of members from Greenleaf expressed their appreciation for our choir's soft and "more meditative" praise songs. My mom, a member of the choir, told me she had been embarrassed to go and sing after hearing how good Greenleaf's choir was. But she was moved by the affirmation from Greenleaf and by the thought that we all really do have something to offer each other. Just as Quaker Gap had laid out a spread for lunch on their turf, so too did Greenleaf cook up fried chicken, barbecue ribs, black-eyed peas, greens, and a table full of desserts. Once again, the fellowship was enjoyed by all—or so the reports came to me, both from Quaker Gap and from Reverend Barber. Indeed, the feelings were so positive that the two churches decided to send our youth groups on a joint mission project the next summer and planned a marriage enrichment retreat for couples from both congregations. That next September, Reverend Barber invited me to come down from Philadelphia and preach at Greenleaf. God, it seemed, was working a miracle of reconciliation between two churches that had been segregated as long as they had been in existence.

But somehow the miracle stopped. There was not a racial explosion, no event where racism reared its ugly head and proved to the black folks from Greenleaf that they really couldn't trust white folks from Klan country. To my knowledge there was never so much as a tense moment between our two churches. We had shared our sermons and songs with each other. We had enjoyed one another's food (not all that different, it turned out). Our youth had learned to appreciate one another, and our married couples had talked intimately about their lives together. We had, you might say, vacationed in one another's worlds. But then it was over. Sure, we kept the pictures in a scrapbook and would look at them from time to time, remembering the good days we had together. And who knows? We might even go back to visit again someday. But I don't think any of us white folks imagined then that there was more to be done for the sake of reconciliation. No one asked whether it made sense for black and white Christians to continue living in our different worlds. That was just the way things were. We were different. But difference wasn't a problem. In a very enlightened way, we had been able to appreciate our differences—even celebrate them. Quaker Gap praised Reverend Barber's "passionate" preaching. Greenleaf lauded our "more meditative" praise songs. We each added our own part to the stew. And life went on. The whites stayed white and the blacks stayed black. After all, that's who we were. We could no more change the color of our skin than a skunk can change its smell. But something had changed. I, for one, had breathed just enough fresh air to know that skunks stink.

Emergence from self-imposed immaturity did not mean salvation—neither for me nor for the body politic in America. The more history I learned, the more I began to doubt the Enlightenment hopes of the West. The Enlightenment vision of a new world order was first born in Europe during the seventeenth and eighteenth centuries when the religious wars that followed the Reformation forced a discussion about how Europeans could live together. At the very same time, an unprecedented age of exploration and discovery brought white Europeans into contact with black and brown bodies from other parts of the world. So just as Europeans were trying to figure out how they could live in peace with one another, they also had to ask how they should relate to these strange dark bodies. Western Christianity was deeply formed by the convergence of these two questions—how to live in peace and how to relate to dark peoples. The discovery of a new world, laden with new economic resources and peopled with unchristian souls, ultimately provided the landscape for a grand experiment to see if the best ideas from the struggle in Europe could make a better social order possible in practice. The name we have given to that experiment is America.

"We hold these truths to be self-evident," the United States Declaration of Independence says, "that all men are created equal and that they are endowed by their creator with certain inalienable rights." The Enlightenment vision that became the hope of America's founding fathers is a call to rise above the differences of particular cultures to recognize those universals that bind all people together. But nearly every black leader in the history of America has pointed out that, as Martin Luther King Jr. said, "America has given the Negro people a bad check, a check that has come back marked 'insufficient funds.'"[4] The so-called universal rights of all people have not been equally applied to black folks in America. The reason is rooted deeply in the history of the Enlightenment vision. As white Europeans encountered the dark bodies of a so-called "new world," they created a spectrum upon which people could be evaluated as more or less "civilized." As might have been expected, the spectrum ran from black to white, with whiteness defining the goal of human society and the essence of civilization. But the problem of race is not as simple as saying that the people who made the rules rigged the game. Even more importantly, the same white minds that created race as a category to define people also suggested for the first time that each race has a contribution to make to human history and universal peace. The vision of a melting pot where "everyone has their part to add to the stew" is inextricably tied to the idea that people with different-colored skin are somehow essentially different from each other. A Southern history of racism, then, does not find its redemption on a Northern college campus or in a New South effort to improve race relations. Instead, it meets its complement there in the story of America. To appeal to the Enlightenment vision of multiculturalism is not to overcome white supremacy but to subtly reinforce the idea of race itself.

At Quaker Gap and Greenleaf we had tried to ask the question, "What does it mean to be one in Christ Jesus?" But we had asked the question in the language of the Enlightenment: "What does it mean for us to appreciate another cultural expression of Christianity?" That way of asking the question not only kept us from facing racial division in the body of Christ as a fundamental problem with our Christianity; it also allowed us white folk to feel good about our efforts to appreciate gospel music and black preaching. Nothing about my church's white theology and practice of Christianity had to change for us to appreciate Greenleaf. We simply assumed that we could move forward from a history of white supremacy to be rounded out by a friendly relationship with people whose lives had been marked by suffering at the hands of white Christians. Yes, we knew we needed to learn from Greenleaf. Many of us from Quaker Gap cried at the thought that we had never worshipped with these brothers and sisters before. But even as we could see our need to appreciate and learn from each other, we were not yet able to imagine that our life together in Christ meant a fundamental rejection of the Enlightenment story that so shaped our American experience.

In the twelfth chapter of Genesis, God speaks to Abram and says, "Leave your country, your people and your father's household and go to the land I will show you.

> "I will make you into a great nation
>   and I will bless you;
> I will make your name great,

and you will be a blessing.
I will bless those who bless you,
and whoever curses you I will curse;
and all the peoples on earth
will be blessed through you." (verses 1-3)

In a fractured world of many peoples, God called one people—Abram's family—to leave their country for a new life in a place unknown to them. To read on through the rest of Scripture is to see how this new people, Israel, is God's plan to redeem all of creation. The salvation of the world depends on this peculiar people, it turns out. When the New Testament writers announce the good news of Jesus, they proclaim that He has somehow fulfilled the promise of Israel. "Do not think that I have come to abolish the Law or the Prophets," Jesus says, claiming continuity with Israel's foundational documents about who they are as a people. "I have not come to abolish them but to fulfill them" (Matthew 5:17). In Jesus, God sums up Israel and brings the history of this people to its great fulfillment: the blessing of all peoples on earth. But God does all this in Jesus of Nazareth, one particular Jew. Just as Abram had to leave everything he knew, forsaking his people, to go to a land God would show him, so also did Jesus invite all to forsake their people so they might become a new humanity in the body of Christ—a people who would bless the whole world, including those they had forsaken for the gospel's sake.

God's plan of salvation, it seems, is a scandal that offends both the insider and the outsider. Jesus' own people could not believe that He would invite anyone and everyone to be part of Israel. Even more important for those of us who are Christian in Gentile America, Jesus calls those outside of Israel to forsake their people and become part of something that none of us can know until God reveals it to us. It is, as the apostle Paul says, a great mystery.

Mysteries are gifts that we must receive and live with long before we understand them. I know this, in part, because I married my friend Leah Wilson (making us both Wilson-Hartgroves) and have lived with her in the mystery of a union that Ephesians says is somehow like the relationship between Jesus and the church. Leah and I were married in the December following September 11, 2001, and found ourselves called to active Christian peacemaking in the midst of a violent world. I wrote in my book *To Baghdad and Beyond* about how we followed Jesus to Iraq at the beginning of America's occupation in March 2003 and witnessed the nonviolent power of God's new humanity. When we were forced to leave Iraq by Saddam's government, we had to drive out through Iraq's western desert while F-16s were still flying overhead and bombing to the left and right of the highway. Just outside of Rutba, one of our cars hit a piece of shrapnel in the road and careened into a side ditch, seriously injuring two of our teammates. Our driver, however, did not immediately recognize that their car was no longer behind us. By the time we turned around to find them, our friends were gone. Their car had been left on its side in the ditch.

Shortly after the wreck, we later learned, a car of Iraqis had stopped by the roadside to help our bloody friends out of the ditch. They took them into their vehicle and carried them to Rutba. There a doctor told them, "Two days ago your country bombed our hospital, but we will take care of you because we take care of everyone. Muslim or Christian, Iraqi or American, we take care of everyone." He sewed up two of our friends' heads, saving their lives. By the time we caught up with them, they were resting in the beds of a makeshift clinic. I asked the doctor what we owed him for his services. "You do not owe me anything," he said. "Please just tell the world what has happened in Rutba."

We came back to the United States in April of 2003, telling that story every chance we could get. The more we told it, the more I realized that it was a modern-day Good Samaritan story. The Iraqis, who were supposed to be our enemies, had stopped by the roadside, picked our friends up out of the ditch, and saved their lives. God used some good Iraqis to show us what it means to "love your neighbor as yourself" (Matthew 22:39). We felt as though we'd learned something important about how God works. He tells us to love our enemies because he uses them to teach us the things we most need to know.

Even as I wrote *To Baghdad and Beyond*, full of the hope that Christian peacemaking was a life-giving response to America's war on terror, I was increasingly aware of a need to go deeper. What was at the root of the horrible violence I had witnessed in Iraq? At the heart of my deeper questions about peacemaking, I began to see, was the theological problem of race: We in America cannot imagine what it might mean for people who are divided to become one in Christ Jesus. Real peace isn't possible until we deal with the division created by the color line.

Slaves in America used to talk about going north, across the Ohio River, as "crossing over Jordan." But I didn't find a promised land in my flight from the South. I couldn't see a way out of the problem of race in the culture of Europe or the education of the North. Back in North Carolina, Quaker Gap and Greenleaf hadn't found a way to overcome segregation either. We knew we needed each other, but we didn't know how to be a people together. In Iraq, though, we'd glimpsed another way: the possibility of learning from the people who were supposed to be our enemies. So when Leah and I packed up our little apartment and headed south to Durham, we made our way to Walltown, a black neighborhood, and got directions to the closest Baptist church. Maybe the only way to find true reconciliation in America was to become disciples of the black church.

CROSSING OVER JORDAN

You were born where you were born and faced the future that you faced because you were black and for no other reason. . . . Please try to be clear, dear James, through the storm which rages about your youthful head today, about the reality which lies behind the words acceptance and integration. There is no reason for you to try to become like white people and there is no basis whatever for their impertinent assumption that they must accept you. The really terrible thing, old buddy, is that you must accept them. And I mean that very seriously. You must accept them and accept them with love. For these innocent people have no other hope. They are, in effect, still trapped in a history which they do not understand; and until they understand it, they cannot be released from it.

James Baldwin, "Letter to My Nephew"

FOUR

Nobody Knows
but Jesus

In 1892, when the trustees of Trinity College decided to move
their institution of higher learning from Randolph County to
the up-and-coming tobacco town of Durham, North Carolina,
George Wall moved with the school. Born a slave in 1856, Mr.
Wall had worked as a custodian at Trinity College ever since his
freedom was secured by Braxton Craven, then president of Trinity
College. On the north side of Trinity's new campus in Durham,
Mr. Wall cut a road into the woods and built a home for his
family. Within walking distance of the campus, Wall worked the
rest of his life as a servant of the college that would become Duke
University.

The historical record isn't clear about just when the name
stuck, but the little community of fellow service workers and
extended family that grew up around Mr. Wall soon came to

be referred to as Walltown. Bounded by Duke's campus on the south, white neighborhoods on the east and west, and a trash dump on the north, Walltown became an island for black folks in a sea of racism that white folks owned. By 1910, members of the Walltown community had established the Wall Street Baptist Church, which, after it was moved to its present location on Onslow Street, became St. John's Missionary Baptist Church. When black children from Walltown faced harassment and abuse walking through the surrounding white neighborhoods to the black elementary school in Hickstown, the community rallied to petition for its own school. The County Board of Education eventually accepted their plan, and the students met in St. John's' building until the new school was constructed.[1]

Leah and I didn't know when we came to Durham that folks in Walltown, many of whom still work for the university, called Duke "the plantation." All I knew about Duke was that they had a good basketball team, I liked some of the books I had read by professors on their faculty, and I had been offered a scholarship to study Christian ministry at their divinity school. When we asked around at Duke about neglected neighborhoods where the church was active in Durham, people told us about Walltown. A few years earlier, three neighborhood churches had partnered with two white churches from adjacent neighborhoods to start Walltown Neighborhood Ministries, a community development and direct aid service center created to address the drug trade, violence, and community deterioration that Walltown had been experiencing since the 1970s. On a landscape that had been racially divided as long as anyone could remember, black and white churches were working together in holistic ministry. God was doing something in the abandoned social space of Walltown, on the margins of those places that "mattered" in Durham. Leah and I decided that

Walltown was where we wanted to be.

But how do a couple of white folks waltz across the lines that race has drawn and join the dance of God's kingdom party? We thought we'd just move to Walltown, but we had decided together with a Hispanic friend, Isaac, to start a house of hospitality, welcoming homeless folks into a spare bedroom or two and sharing life together. The biggest thing we could find for rent in Walltown was a two-bedroom duplex. So we decided to rent a bigger place "just outside" Walltown — that is, just across the Broad Street divide, separating white Old West Durham from black Walltown. We were close enough to walk, we reasoned.

Leah visited Walltown Neighborhood Ministries, where a staff of seven black folks ran an after-school program, a food pantry and emergency assistance program, senior citizen and youth groups, and a health ministry. It seemed like a great place to connect. But they weren't hiring, and it sure didn't look like they'd ever thought of hiring white folk. We didn't have much money in the bank, so Leah and I both needed work. But God was doing something in Walltown. So we decided Leah should just volunteer to help with whatever was needed. If she was supposed to work in Walltown, God could provide money for us to live on.

Meanwhile, I was starting my studies of Bible and theology on "the plantation" at Duke Divinity School. My program called for part-time work in a local church as part of my practical training. So sometime in those first couple of weeks, I met with Duke's director of field education. He explained to me how the Duke family had set up an endowment that paid students generously to work in rural Methodist churches. I told him how I felt called to Walltown and was interested in what the churches there were doing together. "We're about to run out of money," I told him, "but we think God is calling us to Walltown."

Already we had walked over to Walltown's St. John's Missionary Baptist Church a few Sunday mornings. Sylvia Hayes, the director of the Neighborhood Ministry office, was also a minister at St. John's. She had told Leah we were welcome to join them for worship anytime. New to town, we had also accepted invitations from a few other people to worship with them at their churches, so we hadn't settled in yet. But every evening we talked together and prayed about this sense of a call to join God in Walltown. Prayer kept compelling us to say yes to Walltown. St. John's could be our church home, except that the field education office might send me next month to work at some little church an hour and a half outside of Durham. Walltown Neighborhood Ministries looked like the perfect place for Leah to work, except that there was no job there. And we were running out of money fast.

As we waited to hear about my field education placement, we decided we could make it through only one more week without income. The next Monday, Leah was going to take a temp job in an office somewhere and keep looking for something more permanent. But that Friday she came home and told me that two different people who had been working part-time at the Neighborhood Ministry had quit their jobs and that Reverend Hayes had offered her both positions. A couple of weeks later, I got a letter saying that I had been appointed to work as a student minister at St. John's Baptist Church.

We had been attending St. John's for about a month when I saw one of the members walking across Onslow Street one Monday afternoon. "Hey there!" I shouted to her, calling her by name. "Well, hey!" she hollered back. She stopped in the middle of the street and propped her hand on her hip. "Ya'll gonna keep coming back, ain't you?'" she asked with a wry grin.

"If you don't mind," I said.

She slapped her knee and cackled. "It's all right with me, honey!"

White Christians who care about reconciliation often say that we have to start by building relationships with people who aren't like us. And I suppose there is some truth to that. Reconciliation is not possible without relationship. But the woman in her sixties who stopped me on Onslow Street that day already knew something about relating with white folk. Whites and blacks in Durham have never suffered a lack of relationship. A story from the Duke Alumni Register of 1930 recounts how George Wall, then in the seventy-fourth (and last) year of his life, was found early one morning sweeping the porch of a Professor Aldridge's house. "Why, Uncle George, what are you doing here?" someone asked. "Just getting ready for Commencement," Mr. Wall replied. "I always valued 'Uncle George's' type of character," wrote John Franklin Crowell, one-time president of Trinity College. "Value" — an economic term — seems appropriate. Duke's white administration has always benefited from its relationship with Walltown. But however much the racism of the economic order may have been internalized, it must also be said that the relationship was two-sided. Mr. Wall's son, George Frank Wall, told the *Durham Morning Herald* in 1949 that he wanted to "impress on colored men the fine and good relations between Christian white people and Christian Negroes."[2]

Relationships — even "good relations" — between black and white are nothing new in the South. Residents of Walltown who have for three and four generations cleaned toilets, swept floors, and changed bedsheets at Duke University know a lot about relating to white folk. What they know, more than anything, is that white folks don't stick around. However generous and kind they may be on their visits, white folks are always "just visiting." Whether a Duke student tutoring children, a politician working the crowd on community day, or a coworker visiting church on Sunday morning, white folks visit and then they go home. "Ya'll gonna keep coming back?" was a way of asking if we were going to be like every other white person who had ever had a relationship with Walltown. St. John's was sizing us up.

Of course, we were also making our own evaluations of St. John's. Every Sunday after service, Leah and I would ask what the other thought. We began to see the patterns of worship and learn the moves of an unwritten liturgy. Once worship at St. John's was no longer just strange, we started to talk about whether we liked it. More than anything, we were struck by how long and loud the services were. Sometimes the three hours seemed like a joyful celebration of the God who "sits high and looks low." But other times it felt as if we were being beat over the head and told to get up and get excited or you're never going to get out of here. Genuine enthusiasm often raised the decibels on the electric organ and set the people to shouting. But just as often it was anger that got people loud and started them to raging against the Devil and the world and every enemy of what is good. Whatever the motivation, it seemed that she who prayed loudest and longest prayed best. Whoever stomped the floor and shouted "Hallelujah!" was really worshipping. And a sermon wasn't finished until the preacher had yelled at somebody about something.

Leah talked about yelling back inside her head. "Sometimes when I don't agree with what someone is saying, I start thinking about yelling back at them." But she knew that wouldn't be appropriate, so she just yelled inside her head. With the same internalized sense of what is appropriate in cross-cultural situations, I tried to "be myself." Of course I wasn't going to run around or stomp or shout. That wasn't me. But if I could be who I was and they could be who they were and we could all respect our differences, I thought everything would be all right. Besides, to hedge our bets, Leah and I had decided we would also go to a Mennonite church in a neighboring town that meets on Sunday evenings. We felt much more comfortable worshipping there. "It's important for you to have somewhere you can be fed spiritually," a white friend told us. Taking her advice, we at least implicitly acknowledged our doubts: Maybe St. John's wasn't a church we could call home.

For the time being, though, St. John's was my job. One of my responsibilities as a student minister was to help coordinate the play for Black History Month. Reverend Hayes gave me a stack of books and said she wanted a series of scenes to be performed while a tape played some of the great Negro spirituals. She wanted a scene in Africa, with tribal chiefs selling their enemies to slave traders. Then she wanted a scene of bodies piled on top of each other in a ship during the Middle Passage. She wanted a scene from the plantation cotton field and a scene of slaves worshipping in the brush arbor. She really wanted a scene with the white master beating his slave to end with the master hanging a broken black body on the cross. Then she wanted us to turn the congregation into a mass meeting from the Civil Rights Movement for the grand finale. Brother Desi Cooper, who had memorized a number of Martin Luther King's sermons, would recite "I've Been to the Mountain Top," and we would end by singing "We Shall Overcome."

It was when we were rehearsing the mass meeting scene — the performance of white and black worshipping together after scenes of white masters oppressing black slaves — that a minister in the church whom I had come to respect a great deal said to me, "We gotta teach you how this is done. When the man starts preaching, you point your finger and shout, 'Preach!'" I practiced, somewhat timidly: "Preach," I said as I extended my finger slowly. She laughed. I tried again. She said, "You're getting there." Practicing the part that I'd been trying to play for months, I realized for the first time that I had a long way to go. In the eyes of St. John's, it wasn't enough for me to "be me." They didn't want me to worship God my way while they worshipped their way. They wanted to convert me. In a moment of clarity, as I poked my finger at the air and practiced shouting "Preach!" with conviction, I realized that this minister was asking me to become black.

To be black is to know that white Christianity is dangerous. Black slaves who heard the gospel from white preachers in a racist society had to make a distinction between the Christianity of slaveholders and the Christianity of Christ. The Jesus whom white Christians worshipped did not challenge white ownership of fellow human beings as property or even the abuse of Christian brothers and sisters whose black skin marked them as second-class citizens of the kingdoms of God and men. One former slave said, "The professed Christians [in] the South didn't treat their slaves any better than other people, nor so well. I'd rather live with a card player and a drunkard than with a Christian."[3] Black folks who suffered at the hands of white Christians learned to critically assess the Christianity of their oppressors. The Jesus that white folks worshipped was the White Jesus whose picture hung in the dining room of the Big House. He was a sweet and passive Jesus who shepherded His lambs, white as snow. He did not get in the way of political and economic realities but offered Himself, instead, as a substitutionary atonement for sins that stood in the way of eternal life with God. The White Jesus blessed food plucked from the earth and prepared in the kitchen by black hands for the upbuilding and nourishment of white bodies whose actions mattered little because their souls had a home in heaven.

Back in the fields, however, slaves learned to sing, "Everybody talking 'bout heaven ain't going there." Heaven and heaven's God were real, slave Christians reasoned. But the God of Jesus Christ was not blessing the table up at the Big House. The true and living God was in the field and in the brush arbor, suffering with slaves who were surrounded on every side by death. Jesus understood their experience at the bottom of a vicious economic order. So they sang,

Poor little Jesus boy
Made him to be born in a manger
World treated him so mean
Treated me mean too.

For the slave Christian, Jesus was not God's passive payment for sin that could be used as a stamp of approval for the self-interested plans of the privileged. Jesus was born homeless and laid in a manger, had to flee to Egypt as a refugee, associated with prostitutes and sinners, and preached freedom to the poor and imprisoned. As another of the spirituals testified,

Jesus made de dumb to speak.
Jesus made de cripple walk.
Jesus give de blind his sight.
Jesus do most anything.

The image of a sweet shepherd with his lily-white lambs did not acknowledge the ministry that Christ had performed here on earth. Proclaiming the advent of a new social order, Jesus challenged hypocrites, cast money changers out of the temple, and offered the poor and the disinherited the blessing of a new life. Jesus was not crucified because the Sanhedrin and the Roman courts agreed that it would serve the greatest good for Him to die as a sacrifice for humanity's sin; Jesus was crucified by the defenders of the social order because He challenged their authority and insisted that another kingdom was breaking into the world. Black Christians in America had to learn to say that Jesus was not the white god who defended the status quo. No, Jesus was black in America. Every slave who was beaten, every black woman raped, every black man lynched—Jesus was with them all. The Black Christ was God in the human flesh of those who suffered oppression under white supremacy. "Nobody knows the trouble I've seen," black Christians sang. "Nobody knows but Jesus." The Jesus who knew all about their sorrows was black.

In his classic work *A Black Theology of Liberation*, James Cone asserted that "no American theology could even tend in the direction of Christian theology without coming to terms with the black-skinned people of America."[4]

As a white first-year theology student, I was assigned to write a performance of scenes from black history, setting before me the story of black suffering in America. I listened to the tape of the spirituals that would accompany the scenes as I read through books of history I had never been taught, disgusted by the roles that white people played in these stories of inhuman abuse. When it was time to cast the scenes, though, there was only one candidate for all the white roles. I would be the slave trader, ship captain, slave driver and master, as well as Abraham Lincoln and civil rights activist. Before a congregation of black Christians whom we were just getting to know, I was destined to perform my people's terrible past. As we practiced making the sound of a leather whip striking human flesh, I felt sick. Was this really my story? Coming to terms with the history of black-skinned people of America meant confessing that I was the heir of an oppressor people who worshipped a White Jesus. No wonder St. John's was not willing to let me be myself, worshipping God as I knew how to worship. They wanted to introduce me to the true and living God. They wanted to teach me to worship the God who is black.

To worship, though, is to be conformed to the image of what you adore. Worship is always about formation. I'll never forget the time when I was living in Germany that I went with a friend to a Star Trek convention. Now, it must be said, Trekkies are a religious group. They worship the world of the Starship Enterprise. When I went with my friend to the convention, I witnessed the reformation that worship brings about. Germans who otherwise look pretty much like your average American (except that they wear Birkenstock sandals with socks) were suddenly transformed into Klingons. There they were, as seen on TV. They had the funny-looking heads. They wore the uniform. They spoke the language. They inhabited the culture. They were, in short, transformed by a form of worship into the image of what they adored.

The tension Leah and I had been feeling in worship at St. John's was this: We could not worship the Black Christ without becoming black. But becoming black meant forsaking our white identity. We had already begun to feel the questioning glances of white friends and family when we talked about our experience at St. John's. Few people were overtly negative. It was, after all, a good "experience" for us to be having. But so-called "good race relations" depended on our knowing when to leave. Our identity as good white Christians depended on our knowing which lines not to cross. Leah noted that when she was in public with the young black men from the Neighborhood Ministry staff, the questioning gaze of white folks became more intense. As my first term as a student minister at St. John's drew to an end, I felt pressure from some advisors at school to consider my "professional development" and get some experience working in a white church. What if God was calling us to stay at St. John's and make our spiritual home in the black church? It would mean forsaking a white god to worship the Black Christ. But it would also mean forsaking white privilege to become part of a people who live on the underside of the American dream. It might even mean joining with them in God's struggle against white supremacy in America. Were we forsaking our families and white friends if we joined the black church? Were we really up for this? God seemed to be saying that our vacation in the black world was over. Were we going home, or were we here to stay?

In the fifteenth chapter of Matthew's gospel, Jesus is confronted by some Pharisees from Jerusalem about why his disciples don't follow the rules for how good Jews ought to act. Jesus' job as a rabbi was to pass on the identity of His people, Israel, to a new generation. But His elders suspected Him of not guarding the tradition carefully enough. That's why they came to question Him, asking, "Why do your disciples break the tradition of the elders?"

Jesus responds with His own question: "And why do you break the command of God for the sake of your tradition?" The point of tradition, Jesus seems to say, is obedience to God. The only reason anyone should try to be a good Jew is because God has called Israel to be a holy people and has given them the gift of a way of life that does not lead to death. Jesus quotes the prophet Isaiah: "These people honor me with their lips, but their hearts are far from me. They worship me in vain; their teachings are but rules taught by men." It does no good to pay God lip service if you are not actually interested in participating in the radically new social order that God proposes. God is not interested in playing the dummy to some Pharisee's ventriloquist routine. Jesus insists that it does Israel no good to know all the rules if they have not understood the heart of the law — that is, if they have not learned to worship the Lawgiver, the one true God.

Having made His point to the Pharisees, Jesus leaves His accusers standing in Galilee and heads down to the coast of Tyre and Sidon. With the question of what it really means to be God's people on their minds, the disciples (and we readers with them) follow after Jesus, eager to hear more. But before we can catch up with Jesus, a desperate Canaanite woman runs into His path shouting, "Lord, Son of David, have mercy on me! My daughter is suffering terribly from demon-possession." We want to know how to be God's people, but this Gentile woman — this outsider — interrupts our lesson with the rabbi.

The disciples do what we would do. They turn to Jesus (notice they don't even address the crying woman). "Send her away," they say, "for she keeps crying out after us." The disciples want to get rid of this interruption so they can continue their lesson on how to be Israel. And Jesus seems to agree with their sentiment. "I was sent only to the lost sheep of Israel," He says. Jesus remembers the question on our minds: *What does it mean to be God's people? What does it mean to be Israel?* He is not distracted by the cries of this Canaanite woman — this woman who is not Israel, whatever else she is. Jesus is here for the lost sheep of Israel. Jesus is here to show us our identity.

But before Jesus can speak to us, this Canaanite woman cuts in again. Down on her knees now, she begs, "Lord, help me!" From below she makes her request. But Jesus does not bend. "It is not right to take the children's bread and toss it to their dogs," He says. Not only does Jesus show particular concern for the children of Israel, those who have been called to be God's people, but He also maintains the boundaries of Jewish identity by insisting that the Gentile woman at his feet is an outsider. In the common slang of the day, he calls her a dog.

"Yes, Lord," the woman begins in response. She does not complain about being called a dog. She does not demand respect for her cultural identity. She is not thinking about herself. This woman is thinking about her daughter. And she is thinking about Jesus. "Yes, Lord," she says, "but even the dogs eat the crumbs that fall from their masters' table."

This beggar woman is confident that the leftovers from God's table will be enough to supply her needs. Like Lazarus who just wanted the scraps from Dives' table (see Luke 16:19-31), she is a beggar at God's gate. Like Jacob who wrestled God in the Jabbok River's mud, this outsider is saying she will not leave until she is blessed. It may well be that this is the answer Matthew's gospel offers to the question of what it means to be God's people, Israel. "Israel" means the one who has wrestled with God and prevailed. "Woman, you have great faith!" Jesus says to the persistent Canaanite woman. "Your request is granted." That very hour, Matthew says, the woman's daughter was healed. She had wrestled with God and won.

Matthew's story of Jesus and the Canaanite woman is a reminder of God's preferential option for a people. We enlightened souls who believe that all cultures are created equal may want to explain away Jesus' exclusive language in this story. Surely He didn't mean to call the woman a dog. I remember reading a commentary that tried to soften Jesus' apparent ethnocentrism by saying that, in the original language, the word He used actually meant "little dog." Frankly, I don't see how that softens the punch. If the guys who hang out on our street corner call me a "cracker" or a "little cracker," they're saying the same thing: I'm not one of them.

But the good news is that in forsaking her own identity for the sake of her daughter, the Canaanite woman becomes an insider in Matthew's story. Submitting herself to the leadership of one who is strangely other, the Canaanite woman becomes one with Christ. Wrestling with the God of Israel in the man Jesus, she wins by losing—just like Jacob, whom God called Israel. Her witness helps us all to see the humility required to be God's people in the world. This woman must betray her identity as a Canaanite. But in doing so, she becomes a sign for us of the New Israel, where all the peoples of the earth can find their true identity in Christ. This is the heart of reconciliation. But forsaking one's people to become part of God's people is an experience so radical that it tests the limits of human language. Maybe Jesus said it best: You must be born a second time (see John 3:7). "I am not ruling out the rare possibility of conversion among white oppressors, an event that I have already spoken of in terms of white people becoming black," James Cone wrote in his 1975 *God of the Oppressed*. "But conversion in the biblical sense is a radical experience, and it ought not to be identified with white sympathy for blacks or with a pious feeling in white folks' hearts."[5]

The last Sunday in Black History Month at St. John's is African Heritage Sunday. Members are encouraged to wear traditional African attire. After we had been at St. John's a few years, I borrowed a colorful dashiki from a friend and wore it to the service. Afterward, an older woman in the congregation hugged me in the aisle on my way out of the sanctuary and then stood back and exclaimed with feigned formality, "My, that shirt is very becoming!"

"Why, thank you," I replied, and then asked with a hint of

mischief, "What do you reckon I'm becoming?"

"One of us," she said, and she laughed like Sarah laughed when God said she would bear a child in her old age. New life when we least expect it — it is the signature of Israel's God. That God, I had to learn, is black in America. The biblical God who chooses to marry a people looked down on America and saw an economic order that claimed to own black bodies, political documents that counted black people as fractions, a culture that insisted black minds were inferior, and a beauty myth that trained eyes to see black features as unattractive. God saw how America surrounded black life with death on every side. And God said to black folk, "You will be my people, and I will be your God."

It is true that nobody knows the collective suffering of black folks in America — not even the black individual who has experienced her own personal suffering. She sings the old song to remember how much greater the collective suffering of her people has been and to situate her own struggle within that history. "Nobody knows the trouble I seen . . ." She is telling the truth about a people bound by death from the shipholds of the Middle Passage to the dehumanization of chattel slavery to the Jim Crow South and the Northern ghettoes to gang violence and the formation of a black criminal caste. "Nobody knows . . ." she sings. "Nobody knows but Jesus."

But Jesus does know. Jesus knows because the Black Christ testifies that God has been with this people all along, suffering with them through the Valley of the Shadow of Death and struggling with them for a new world where, as the prophet Amos wrote, "let justice roll on like a river, righteousness like a never-failing stream!" (5:24). This is the new world that we must die to enter into. But it is a world of life — divine life — filled with holy laughter at a God who never ceases to surprise.

Leah and I decided to ask St. John's for membership in their body because we wanted to be part of that life. Yes, we had to count the cost. And we knew there would be costs that we didn't yet know how to count, for ourselves and for our children. But even if it cost everything, we knew this life was worth it. Jesus already knew the troubles we would see. And Jesus would be with us all the way.

FIVE

I Want Jesus to Walk with Me

"**H**ospitality is central to . . . reconciliation," says Robert Schreiter in his book *The Ministry of Reconciliation*. "So much of the ministry of reconciliation is about waiting and listening. . . . Hospitality, on the other hand, is something we can do. Here we can take the initiative to create an environment in which reconciliation can happen."[1] As we waited for a way into Walltown, before we found a home at St. John's, Leah and I rented a house together with our friend Isaac and set up an extra bedroom to welcome the stranger we hoped God would send. Leah explained to Reverend Hayes that we wanted to be a house of hospitality and that we had set aside a "Christ room" for someone who needed a place to stay. "For . . . I was a stranger and you invited me in," Jesus said (Matthew 25:35). We wanted the chance to host Jesus in our home.

Reverend Hayes said she knew two or three people who might be interested in coming to stay with us. She told Leah about Jerry, who had been paying fifty bucks a week to stay on a friend's couch in Walltown. Now the friend was getting evicted and Jerry had no place to go. Leah, Isaac, and I went to visit Jerry the next day at his friend's place. When he invited us into the duplex, we saw that the electricity had already been shut off and most of the furniture was gone. The landlord said that everything else had to be out of the apartment by the end of the day. Jerry needed somewhere to go. We invited him to come stay with us.

So within two weeks of starting our little experiment in hospitality as a Christian community, we were a white woman, a white man, a Hispanic man, and a black man trying to figure out how to live together. We called our community Rutba House, after the little town of Rutba in Iraq. We wanted to remember what we had learned about how God shows us His love through a Good Samaritan, one who's supposedly our enemy. We thought it was a parable for how hospitality could be an act of peacemaking, the first step toward reconciliation. It was a story we wanted to remember in our life together at Rutba House.

But outside of a war zone, reconciliation seemed to be about negotiating a thousand little differences in our life together. Leah and I had been vegetarians since we were married, mostly because we wanted to conserve resources. In college we had learned about our "ecological footprint" and the Christian's responsibility to care for creation. Isaac, who had also thought quite a bit about how to eat like a Christian, was fairly convinced that people never would have eaten animals if Adam and Eve had not rebelled against God in the Garden of Eden, so he tried to be a vegan in celebration of God's new creation. But Jerry thought all this talk about God and food sounded a little funny. He said that if meat were available, we ought to thank the Lord and fry it up.

And that was just our conversation about food. We also shared a bathroom, tried to pray together, kept a common account, and decided how to spend our money together. We split up chores to keep the house going and committed to making decisions about our life together by consensus. If we were going to find unity with such different backgrounds, we would have to learn how to talk through our disagreements. We would have to learn how to speak the truth in love.

Part of telling the truth meant admitting that we weren't all on equal footing. Leah, Isaac, and I had welcomed Jerry, believing that we should receive our guest as Christ. It was an honor to host him. But that still meant we were hosts and he was a guest. We wanted to build trust by sharing household responsibilities and decision making, but Jerry made it clear that he wanted to move on as soon as he could get on his feet and save enough money to rent his own place. While we were still trying to find a way into Walltown, Jerry told us how glad he was to have gotten out. Just across the Broad Street divide between our two neighborhoods, he saw new possibilities. In a few months, he hoped to have a place of his own — outside Walltown.

We did what we could to drive Jerry to job interviews, get him dress clothes for catering jobs, and help him save money. "Transitional housing" seemed like a fair description of our new hospitality ministry. We would be a community that hosted people on their way out of prison, addiction, and hard times. We would offer a safe space, encourage guests, and connect them to resources on their way to independence. But all of our effort to help Jerry transition meant he was becoming less and less a part of the community. He worked in the evenings when we were home. He reported his progress at house meetings, and we listened like experts, ready to share our wisdom. Instead of growing closer in community, we drifted further and further from each other into the roles of guest and hosts.

One day Isaac asked me if I had driven his car recently. We shared our cars freely, but I knew I hadn't driven his in some time. He told me he knew he had left it with three-quarters of a tank of gas and that it was on empty when he got back in it. Unless there was a leak in the tank, someone had driven his car. A lot. Jerry didn't have a license, so we had never given him keys to either of our cars. When we were able, we gave him rides. Often he took the bus. But we knew it might have been tempting for him to drive one of our cars when we weren't around. We decided to be more careful about leaving our keys lying around the house.

Not long after that, I got in our car one day, cranked up the engine, and smelled cigarette smoke. Leah and I didn't smoke. But Jerry did. I looked down at the dashboard and saw the fuel hand on empty. We had a problem we needed to talk about. So that night when Jerry came home, we asked him if he could join us in the living room for a house meeting. We sat down in the living room and explained what had happened. We told Jerry that we had been careful to keep our keys with us, so we knew that whoever had driven the car had made a copy of the key. We talked about how trust was important if we were going to live together. We said that we were ready to forgive him for taking the cars without asking and driving them without a license or insurance. Then, finally, we asked him if he had driven the cars.

"I know it looks like everything points to me," he said, "but all I can say is I didn't do it. I couldn't stand to look ya'll in the face if I had done something like that."

For the next week and a half, Jerry avoided us like the plague. We had another meeting or two to try to talk about the cars, but we got nowhere. We didn't trust Jerry, and he clearly didn't trust us. He tried to be upbeat. We tried to be nice. But we all knew we couldn't go on like that. After four months of life together, Jerry decided it was best to just leave. He called us from his girlfriend's house to say that he'd decided to stay with her. And that's the last we heard from him. When Leah drove past him on the street a few weeks later, she blew the horn and waved, but Jerry just kept walking, as if he had never seen our baby blue Toyota.

"Deception," wrote Howard Thurmond, "is perhaps the oldest of all the techniques by which the weak have protected themselves against the strong. Through the ages, at all the stages of sentient activity, the weak have survived by fooling the strong."[2] It was true on the plantation, where slaves stole from the Big House to have enough to feed their kids at home. It was true under Jim Crow, when separate wasn't equal and "getting by" meant getting what you could, even if the law said it wasn't yours. And it was true at the Rutba House, where, whether we admitted it or not, we had power and Jerry did not. Sure, it was wrong to lie. Jerry knew that as well as any of us. But Jerry also knew that he had crossed a line on Durham's landscape. He wasn't in Walltown anymore. He was on the other side of Broad Street. Here he was living with students from "the plantation" in a "good neighborhood." Of course, Jerry had been across Broad Street before, just like he had been over to Duke to cater events and to the fancy hotels downtown to prep food in the kitchen. But he knew that what was on the other side wasn't his. It belonged to people who had power. It belonged to people like us.

Our attempt to overcome a history of racial division by simply inviting Jerry into our home had failed miserably. It had failed despite our best intentions, despite our greatest hopes, despite consistent prayer and earnest belief in the power of Christ to transform broken relationships. It had failed because of a lie. But it wasn't the little lie that Jerry told. Yes, his lie was sin. Yes, it hurt us. And yes, it hurt Jerry. But his lie was almost inevitable. Jerry's lie was a survival tactic, learned and practiced on the underside of an exploitative economic system. Jerry's deception was the practiced technique of the weak, employed to protect himself against a powerful system of lies that said his life was not worth as much as mine because of the color of his skin. Jerry's little lie was the result of a much bigger lie—a lie so big that we assumed it was just the way things were. We hadn't accounted for the fact that our very location outside of Walltown was conditioned by that bigger lie. We'd thought honest relationships in community would be enough to overcome the dividing lines of Durham. But we had missed the reality that any realtor could see: We were living on the west side of Broad Street because we weren't black.

In their study *Divided By Faith: Evangelical Religion and the Problem of Race in America*, sociologists Michael Emerson and Christian Smith interviewed evangelical Christians to see how faith affected views of racial division and inequality. After a national survey and hundreds of face-to-face interviews, Emerson and Smith concluded that evangelical faith inspires white Christians to desire racial reconciliation. And, at the same time, "evangelicals' application of their cultural tool kit, in the context of inter-group isolation, unwittingly contributes to the reproduction of racial inequality."[3] That's what the study found. Even though we want to overcome racism, we end up reinforcing it by the way we live. There is a problem deep in the heart of American evangelicalism. We are caught in a contradiction, always getting in the way of the very thing we long for. It's the sort of study that makes you feel a little sick to your stomach.

One of the things Emerson and Smith observe about

evangelicals is that almost all of us believe that personal relationships are the way to overcome prejudice. Reconciliation is about people, so it happens between people, we say. Hearts are changed when we forgive and are forgiven in relationship. After all, "racism" is just a big idea to explain why some people have been separated from other people in a history of sin. Jesus came to overcome that sin. So the tragedy, we want to say, isn't that white people hate black people, but that we don't know them. If only we could get to know each other, racism could be defeated.

But in their chapter "Let's Be Friends," Emerson and Smith write that "like their forebears during Jim Crow segregation, who prescribed kindness toward people of other races and getting to know people across races but did not challenge the Jim Crow system, present-day white evangelicals attempt to solve the race problem without shaking the foundations on which racialization is built."[4] We assume that close relationships will be enough to overcome the dividing power of race. But the problem is not that blacks and whites in America have not had close relationships; the problem is that we've inherited five hundred years of unjust and abusive relationships based upon a lie.

A local pastor told me about visiting a slave castle when he was in Ghana. These castles on the coast of Africa were "processing centers" for black men and women who were about to make the Middle Passage and become slaves in the "new world." This pastor says you can still smell the stench of human waste in those dungeons where living black bodies were piled up like cargo. Above the dungeons there is a viewing room. Here European traders forced women and men alike to stand naked so they could evaluate the economic worth of their bodies. But these evaluations were never strictly business transactions. The pastor told me he looked down through the hole above the women's dungeon, where slave traders could go after their work was done to select a sex partner for the evening. He looked down into the darkness and almost threw up. Maybe it was the stench. But I think he also felt in his gut the injustice of forced intimacy.

The colonial economic project that stole land from Native Americans and forced black slaves to work that land did not disallow relationships between blacks and whites. For hundreds of years in America it was normal and acceptable for white men to own black bodies. A "mammy" raised white children, feeding them from her black breasts. And a black maid served as confidante to her master's wife, listening to her most intimate confessions as she brushed her hair. No doubt, blacks and whites have had more of a relationship in modern America than they ever had before. But it is a relationship built on the economic lie of white ownership — an "ownership" that extended even to other people's bodies.

Of course, white people don't own black bodies anymore. And we haven't for a long time. We like to believe that the oppressive economic reality of slavery is far behind us and that its ugly truth doesn't touch on our lives today. I grew up in post–civil rights America, getting a day off school for Martin Luther King Jr.'s birthday and believing that his dream had been achieved in the colorblind eyes of the law. But the truth is that as of 1994, the median income of blacks in America was 62 percent of whites — which is roughly the same economic disparity that existed before the Civil Rights Movement.[5] And that's just looking at income. When you look at total net worth — the value of what someone owns minus what they owe in debts — the average black person in America today is worth 8 percent of his or her white "equal."[6] The economic lie of white ownership is alive and well.

When we invited Jerry to come live with us, we said we wanted to welcome him as Christ. I'm not sure we knew what we meant by that. I mean, we were trying to say that he was a child of God. We wanted to believe that the new family we'd been grafted into at St. John's wasn't just a spiritual reality, but that it made a real difference in the world. If Jerry was our brother, why shouldn't we be able to live together, trust one another, and walk beside each other in life? Like the song we sing at St. John's says,

> I want Jesus to walk with me
> I want Jesus to talk with me . . .
> Step by step all the way.

If Jerry was Christ to us, I guess we just thought we wanted to walk and talk with him. But we didn't think much about what he might say. I never anticipated that he, like Jesus on the road to Emmaus, would become a stern teacher, saying essentially, "How foolish you are" (Luke 24:25) and opening our eyes to see how a history of economic injustice had shaped the land we were living on. Like Jesus, Jerry had vanished just about the time we were beginning to recognize him for who he really was. And we were left with a truth burning in our hearts, wondering what to do next.

"Ya'll just don't know how good it feels to get out of Walltown." More than anything else, that's what we remembered Jerry saying. But this talk about "getting out" troubled us. Something about it seemed to reinforce the problem. God had called us to Walltown not to help black folk get out and make it in a world that white folk own, but to learn from the black church how to imagine a whole new world—a world in which God owns the cattle on a thousand hillsides and longs for all of his children to have enough. We weren't called to be a rescue station on the dividing line, offering access to white power (and inviting deception from those who knew by experience that they couldn't have it). God wanted us to settle down in the space that had been abandoned by the white establishment—to live as guests in a neighborhood that black folks owned. God wanted us to move to Walltown.

But by the time we'd decided to cross over the Broad Street divide, another guy from Walltown was already living with us. Raymond had met us in Walltown before Jerry left. He'd heard about our house and told us that if we ever had an opening, he'd love to fill it. He was living with his mother at the time, a woman who volunteered a lot at the Neighborhood Ministry and had befriended Leah. She told Leah how hard it was for her to live with her grown son in a little duplex. So Raymond wanted out, his momma wanted him out, and we had a space for him to move into. About all we'd known when Jerry left was that we didn't know what we were doing. But we'd invited Raymond to come anyway. We would try to figure it out together.

We asked Raymond at a house meeting whether he thought it made sense for us to move to Walltown. "Hell, no!" he said. "I just got out of there. Why would I want to go back?" We'd said we wanted to have more honest conversations with guests. So far so good. I tried to explain what we thought we had learned from Jerry. Raymond listened, but he knew all too well what the world looked like from the other side. He knew the desperation of having no options and the dehumanization of being criminalized for pursuing the options you have. He'd also been disappointed by church folk who talked a good talk but drove home to the suburbs after church on Sunday and forgot the reality of the streets. Raymond was as glad to be out of Walltown as Jerry had been. And it was hard to blame him.

But walking across Broad Street on our way to St. John's each

Sunday, I kept thinking about the lie of that dividing line and the economic reality it represented. We walked into Walltown to sing the songs of Zion with saints who knew about how God had brought them "a mighty long way." They would shout at the top of their lungs, thanking God for waking them up and giving them air to breathe. The words of worship lifted us above the Broad Street divide, our history of enmity, wealth disparity, and the need for deception. But when the preacher was finished preaching and the choir was finished singing their final hallelujahs, we'd walk back across Broad Street to our home on the other side. We'd walk past the young guys in white T-shirts and baggy pants standing on the corner. Holding my Bible in one hand, I'd wave with the other. And keep walking. I couldn't help but wonder how God's kingdom could come on earth as it is in heaven if the white folks go home to their white neighborhoods and the black folks who can follow them, while the poor stand on the street corner, waiting until "justice rolls down like a river, righteousness like a never-failing stream" (Amos 5:24). I longed for a social space where what we said in worship could become an economic and political reality.

The book of Exodus begins with a list of the names of the children of Israel who'd gone down to live in Egypt when there was a famine in Canaan. Just as God blessed Adam and Eve in the garden and said, "Be fruitful and increase in number" (Genesis 1:28), Exodus says that the children of Israel were "fruitful and multiplied greatly and became exceedingly numerous, so that the land was filled with them" (Exodus 1:7). God's beloved community was thriving in Egypt land. But this worried Pharaoh, the commander-in-chief of the world's greatest superpower. He had to think about national security. *What if a war breaks out?* he asked himself. "All these Israelites might actually be terrorists, ready to join with the enemy forces and destroy our way of life." So Exodus says that Pharaoh decided to "deal shrewdly" with Israel (Exodus 1:10). He put taskmasters over them and made them into slaves.

It's worth noting that Pharaoh made the children of Israel into slaves because he was afraid of them. Intricate theories may have been devised to explain why Hebrews were inferior to Egyptians and thus deserved the hard labor of building pyramids. Perhaps among the intellectuals of that great civilization there were even scientific explanations of the biological differences between these two peoples. But if there were, that all happened after the fact. The Bible says that the children of Israel were made slaves because Pharaoh was afraid of them. So afraid, in fact, that he ordered the partial-birth abortion of all the male children of Israelite women. The economy of Egypt had become a system of death for the young Hebrew man. That's why Moses wasn't supposed to be alive.

But people who live under a system of death develop tactics of survival, often subverting the framework they inhabit from within. Pharaoh had decreed that all male children be thrown into the Nile. That was the official order. So Moses' mother threw him into the Nile, just as she was told. But first she put him in a basket, made waterproof with bitumen and pitch. She followed the letter of the law, even while, hope against hope, she sought to subvert its spirit of death. And sure enough, Moses survived. He floated downriver and just so happened to get caught up in the river grass by the spot in the Nile where Pharaoh's daughter went down to bathe. She sent her maids over to see what was in the basket, and when they brought back a little Hebrew child, she decided to raise it as her own. In her father's house. Talk about crossing a social divide. She called him Moses, which means "drawn out of the water." Here was one who had made it out.

So Moses grew up on the other side, together with his Hebrew mother, whom Pharaoh's daughter conscripted as a house slave to take care of this child that she claimed as her own. No doubt, Moses had access to the power of Egypt's domination system. We have no record of his education, his cultural training, or his formation in the ranks of the social elite. Nor does Exodus tell us anything about how a relationship with a Hebrew woman and her child affected Pharaoh's daughter, except to say that nothing changed. The intimacy of real relationship between oppressor and oppressed in the White House of Egypt did nothing to change the system of domination. We know this because Exodus says that when Moses was a grown man, he went out to his people and saw one of them being beaten by an Egyptian taskmaster.

Down from the Big House, Moses saw firsthand the death dealing that was happening in the fields. And he was outraged. He killed the oppressive Egyptian and buried him in the sand, hoping no one had seen him. But when he went out the next day, no doubt eager to look further into the injustices that were happening among his people, Moses found two Hebrews fighting one another. "Break it up!" he shouted. "Why are you beating up your brother?" One of the slaves turned to him and replied, "What, are you going to kill us like you killed that guy yesterday?" And Moses went silent. No doubt, his position in the Big House was precarious as he teetered between the good graces of a powerful woman and the fickle will of a fearful ruler. Now he knew the word was out. The guest in the White House had not only lied but also killed. "When Pharaoh heard of this," Exodus says, "he tried to kill Moses" (2:15). But Moses was already gone.

Gone to the desert, to the dry and abandoned space. There beyond the all-seeing eye of an oppressive economy that, to this day, gazes down from the top of an Egyptian pyramid on the back of our one-dollar bill—there Moses learns who he is. Moses: the one who has been drawn out of the waters. We who associate water with beach vacations have to discipline ourselves to hear Moses' name with biblical ears. "Waters" in Scripture are not the playground of surfers; they are the powers of death. "In the beginning God created the heavens and the earth," Genesis begins. ". . . The Spirit of God was hovering over the waters" (1:1-2). Over the chaos and nothingness of the waters, God flutters like a dove. And when God speaks, the words are, "Let there be an expanse between the waters to separate water from water" (1:6).

In the midst of the chaos, God carves out a space for life and the beloved community. But when the human community turns against God and one another, God opens up the heavens and the fountains of the deep, and a great flood covers the earth, killing every living thing except for Noah's family and the animals that were with them in the ark. The rainbow is God's promise that earth will never again be destroyed by waters. But the waters become a symbol for those forces that always threaten to destroy life. "If the LORD had not been on our side," the psalmist cries out, ". . . the flood would have engulfed us, the torrent would have swept over us, the raging waters would have swept us away" (124:1,4-5). The waters represent the power of the Enemy.

But Moses is the one who was drawn out of the waters. He was rescued from Egypt's death system and given a new life. Of course, Pharaoh's daughter, who gave Moses his name, considered herself his savior. She drew him out of the water. She offered him a new life in her father's house. She gave him access to power in a world that would have preferred him dead. But that assimilation into the domination system proved disastrous for Moses. Now he is in the abandoned space. Here Moses learns who he is and who it really was that drew him out.

Moses' self-understanding is clear when he has a son together with Zipporah, whom he met when she was drawing water (that's a little biblical humor). Moses names his son Gershom, "saying, 'I have become an alien in a foreign land'" (Exodus 2:22). In the desert, Moses sees that Egypt is not his home. Whether working the fields or working his relationships in the Big House, Moses had been an alien to Egypt's domination system. He had been both the near-victim of Egypt's violence at his birth and the executioner of it in a moment of rage. But that economy of domination and violence was not his home. Maybe Pharaoh's daughter had rescued Moses from the waters of the Nile, but the Lord God had rescued him from the "waters" of an economic system that required the forced labor of many to support the unchecked desires of a few. Out in the desert, speaking from a burning bush, God tells Moses that He means to draw His whole people out through the waters of the Red Sea—but not before He makes clear to the Egyptians that their waters represent death by turning the Nile into blood. In the end, it turns out, all those who are so addicted to Egypt's system that they will fight with Pharaoh to defend it will be buried under the waters of the Red Sea. The whole system of death will come crashing down on them.

In the desert Moses sees that he has been drawn out of Egypt's economy. And in the same abandoned space, after Moses has led Israel out of Egypt, God speaks through him to teach the people about a new economy. In chapter 16 of Exodus, after the people have forgotten the horror of Egypt's economy and begun to wish they could go back, Moses informs them that God is going to rain bread from heaven. But they are to take enough for only today. In this new economy God promises to provide enough for everyone. The Israelites no longer have to scrounge for scraps at the Big

House and steal them away to feed their children. In God's just community, there is enough for everyone.

"The Israelites did as they were told," Exodus says. "Some gathered much, some little. And when they measured it by the omer, he who gathered much did not have too much, and he who gathered little did not have too little. Each one gathered as much as he needed" (Exodus 16:17-18). So the desert became a school for God's economy. There Israel learned the just order of divine distribution. There they learned how Egypt had denied them dignity and crushed their very lives. But there they also began to dream of a kingdom where there would be enough for everyone to have what they need. God taught them about a day of Sabbath rest, and a year when the produce of the fields would be left to feed the poor in the land. After seven sets of Sabbath years, the fiftieth year was to be a Jubilee, when debts would be forgiven, prisoners set free, and land returned to the families it was originally allotted to in the just distribution. In this new economy there would be enough for everyone—even the undocumented worker. "Do not oppress an alien," God said. "You yourselves know how it feels to be aliens, because you were aliens in Egypt" (Exodus 23:9). God's people are to be a living alternative to the corrupt economy of Egypt.

Like Moses at the burning bush, our roommate Raymond didn't want to go back. He'd gotten out of Walltown, and he'd just as soon stay out. Raymond half thought he'd been drawn out, saved from the raging waters of an economy that had nearly killed him. But he wasn't that naïve. Raymond knew that Broad Street ran not between two economies but between two spheres of a divided kingdom. The same system of domination controlled both white and black Durham. But Walltown was the place where the system did its death dealing. Walltown was the abandoned space. Given the options, Raymond thought it best to stay out.

Raymond's story wasn't unlike John Perkins', founder of the Christian Community Development Association (CCDA), who grew up the son of sharecroppers in rural Mississippi during the 1930s and '40s. Perkins learned early in his life that the economic system of the South was stacked against him. He tells a story about how, when he was twelve years old, he worked all day hauling hay for a white man only to be paid fifteen cents — a tenth of the going rate for a day's labor. Perkins writes about what it felt like to realize there was nothing he could do about it:

> I took a long look at what had just happened to me and really began thinking about economics. That man had the capital: the land and the hay. And he had the means of production: the wagon and the horses. All I had were my wants and needs — and my labor. So I was exploited. . . . From that day on I began to understand something about the economic system and how it worked.[7]

Four years later, when Perkins was sixteen, his older brother Clyde was shot by a white police officer and died in Perkins' arms on the way to the hospital. Once again, there was nothing he could do about it. Rage welled up within him, and he knew that if he stayed he would lash out like Moses had against the Egyptian taskmaster and kill a white man. So Perkins fled, all the way to California. There he made a life for himself. With the labor of his hands, he earned money and saved it. Soon he had enough capital to buy a house. "By the spring of 1957, I could feel I had pretty good chances in life," Perkins writes. "And that good feeling was a lot deeper than just the money I was able to earn. I was a provider for my family, I was a man. And I was going places!"[8]

Then Perkins had his own burning bush experience. He understood for the first time that if he were crucified with Christ, Jesus could come and live inside of him (see Galatians 2:20). But as he began to walk with Jesus, Perkins heard God calling him back to Mississippi. Back to the place where he'd been humiliated at the end of a hard day's work. Back to the place where a white man had shot his brother dead. Back to the abandoned place. But why? Why go back? Perkins wasn't sure why in 1960. But after fifteen years back in Mississippi, he could see more clearly:

> Whether or not we admit it, our reading of biblical ethics is colored by our perception of the world around us. If we think that there are only a few "bad guys" such as burglars and murderers, and that all the given political, legal and economic structures around us are basically okay, then we are bound to read our Bibles in a certain way. We will assume that it tells us to "lay low," whether we are a part of the law or only under the law; that the person who speaks out is a rebellious agitator.
>
> But that assumption can be badly shaken up by a good look at what happens to many people who are simply crushed by, rather than helped by, these social structures and institutions we take for granted. If sin can exist at every level of government, and in every human institution, then also the call to biblical justice in every corner of society must be sounded by those who claim a God of Justice as their Lord.[9]

God called Perkins back to Mississippi to teach him about an economy where the waters don't mean death, but where "justice rolls on like a river, righteousness like a never-failing stream"

(Amos 5:24). Out of that journey CCDA was born, an association of Christians who heard the gospel Perkins was preaching and relocated to abandoned inner cities and rural coal towns in order to read the Bible anew. From the streets of Sandtown in Baltimore to the hills of Appalachia, people who knew themselves to be aliens in a strange land were trusting Jesus' promise that "the time has come and the kingdom of God is near" (see Mark 1:15). In economic deserts they were learning to see through the lies of Egypt's domination system to the reality of redistribution in Christian community development.

For Isaac, Leah, and me, the journey was messy. We told Raymond about what we thought we'd learned from Jerry. We told him about John Perkins and the Christian Community Development Association. We talked and we talked and we talked. But he still didn't want to go back. Then one day Leah came home ecstatic that she had found a house for rent in Walltown that wasn't split up into a duplex but had five bedrooms. We all went over and looked at it. It was perfect for hospitality, and just behind St. John's, on a street we didn't usually drive down. "Well, if ya'll want to move," Raymond said, "I guess I'll move with you." Two weeks later we put everything we owned on a flatbed trailer and fled across Broad Street into Walltown.

We showed up with an adrenaline rush, sure that God had opened the door for us to move into this house. But the neighbors on Berkeley Street greeted us with silent stares. Though some of them had seen us walk by on our way to St. John's, they didn't know who we were or why we had come. All they could see was that we were white. If we weren't there to buy drugs, they weren't sure why we were there. So we tried to be nice (we weren't just white folk; we were excited white folk). We said hello, asked folks how they were doing, and introduced ourselves as the new neighbors down the street. People were cordial. Most of them smiled a half smile and replied, "Nice to meet you," in their best "civilized" accents. But nothing more. Those everyday interactions were inevitably interrupted by an awkward pause, and then abruptly cut off. "Well, all right . . . I'm going to get on in the house. Have a good day."

Of course, they had questions—questions like, "What are you white folk doing here?" and "What do ya'll want from us?" And we had questions too. We had a thousand questions. We'd come to Walltown to learn, after all. But all of us, black and white, knew not to ask our questions. They revealed too much about our mutual awareness of a tension that felt too strong to overcome.

At home Raymond started schooling us. "Ya'll know what they're thinking, don't you? They think the cops put you over here to rat out the drug dealers." We'd crossed the dividing line, but we were still people who belonged on the other side. We were more likely to be undercover cops than friendly neighbors. "Or they think Duke put ya'll over here," Raymond said. Another real possibility. A few years earlier Duke had bought up four blocks just south of us and redeveloped them with $400K to $500K houses for faculty and staff to live in. Maybe "the plantation" was trying to expand its territory and we were the advance guard. Some of this Raymond had heard people say, some he was just speculating, but all the possibilities were suspicious. White folk in Walltown had to be up to no good.

Whatever doubts he still had about moving back into the neighborhood, though, Raymond started speaking up for us to the neighbors. "The government didn't send them in here," he'd say. "They went over to Iraq to protest the government." So some folks started asking about Iraq. We told the story of how we'd received hospitality in Rutba and said we named our house after the town because we wanted to learn to live with that same kind of love. Raymond translated: "We're here because we care about the neighborhood," he started saying. And when he said it, a new "we" began to form. Raymond wasn't our guest anymore. We were on his turf, and he had become our teacher, advocate, and host.

"They all right," he'd say to the neighbors. And conversations started to happen. We talked politics, discussed the news, told stories about where we came from, and got to know each other's families. It turned out most of those folks on our block cared about the neighborhood too. So we started talking about our concerns. We knew we were only at the beginning of a long conversation. But the "we" had changed. Raymond's welcome made it possible for us to begin to walk beside our neighbors. On the streets and around the dinner table, we started walking and talking together. And I began to see the world around me with new eyes.

At the end of Luke's story about the two folks walking with Jesus on the road to Emmaus, it says that when they got to the town, Jesus acted as though He was going to keep walking down the road, but they "urged him strongly, 'Stay with us, for it is nearly evening; the day is almost over'" (Luke 24:29). Maybe it was because they knew they had more to learn from Jesus. Or maybe it was because they didn't want Him to be out on the streets alone at night. Whatever the case, they asked Jesus to be their guest. And He accepted the invitation.

But no sooner than they were inside, Jesus sat down at the head of the table, "took bread, gave thanks, broke it and began to give it to them" (verse 30). He started serving the meal, just like He had served it to His disciples in the Upper Room. The guest made Himself the host. And that's when Luke says, "Their eyes were opened" (verse 31). That's when they recognized Jesus. That's when they knew the Resurrection was real. And that's when they began to understand that if Christ is risen, the whole world is changed. The way things are is not the way things have to be. Not even in Walltown.

SIX

I Know It Was the Blood

Isaac, Leah, and I spent the summer after we moved into the neighborhood working for Reverend Hayes at Walltown Neighborhood Ministries. We helped run a summer camp for neighborhood kids, made runs to the local food bank, organized meetings to discuss community concerns, and visited with folks on their front porches. As "community ministers," we also responded to people who called in for help because their husband was beating them or their son had AIDS or they saw some young guys hiding drugs under their porch. We'd take down the caller's address and head out to see what we could do. But before we could get out the door, Reverend Hayes would stop us. She'd call us all together, have us hold hands in a circle, and begin to pray. "I plead the blood of Jesus," she'd shout, gripping my hand while swaying back and forth. Then she would name the demons that she saw at work in the situation. "I plead the blood of Jesus over the spirit of fear. Hallelujah! I renounce the spirit of addiction and call out the spirit of anger. Yes, God!" She talked to the spirits as if they were standing in front of her. And she talked like she was mad at them. "In the name of Jesus, I rebuke you!" When she really got fired up, Reverend Hayes would shout something I couldn't understand, stomp her feet on the ground, and call down the power of God to set the captives free. She always ended by thanking God that He had already answered her prayer. Then she would let us go.

On the last Friday of June that summer, after Isaac had been out on a call, he drove home to Rutba House for lunch. As he turned onto Berkeley Street, just half a block from our house, he watched a man in the car in front of him reach out of his tinted window with a pistol in his hand and open fire at the guys standing on the corner. The guys hit the ground as the car sped away. Isaac jerked his car over to the side of the street. "Are you guys okay?" he asked as he jumped out of his car. "Yeah, yeah, we're fine," they said, brushing themselves off. One guy named Robert was holding his elbow, and Isaac saw that it was bleeding. "You sure you're okay?" Isaac asked. "Yeah," he said, still holding his elbow and grimacing. Together with the other guys from the corner, Robert walked down the street, got in a car, and drove away.

That was on Friday. Saturday the guys weren't hanging out on the corner. All in all it was a quiet day. But as I was brushing my teeth before going to bed, I heard shots go off like firecrackers outside. I could see down to the corner from our bathroom window, but there was no one visible underneath the streetlight. *Maybe it was firecrackers*, I thought. Then I went to bed.

Next day was a beautiful, clear Sunday, and we went over to

worship at St. John's. We sang and prayed and worshipped the Lord "in the beauty of holiness" (see 1 Chronicles 16:29, KJV). Somebody thanked God for waking her up that morning because "it could have been the other way." And after the service I walked out into the afternoon sunshine, thanking God for the beauty of creation and looking forward to lunch. But when we got out to the parking lot, I saw that our street was blocked off and lined with cop cars. Neighbors were out on their porches and standing in groups on the sidewalk. We asked what was going on and somebody said, "Lil' Robert's dead."

I remember a neighbor sitting on her porch, staring hard down the street as though she were watching the Devil himself. "I know'd somebody was dead," she said. "I know'd it when I heard the dogs howlin'. Dogs will bark when they hear something at night. But they only howl like that when somebody's dying." When Robert hadn't come home the night before, his momma and his girlfriend went out looking for him. They checked the hospitals and walked the streets all night. But it wasn't until Sunday morning that his momma, Mary, found Robert lying facedown in the ditch behind Ms. June's house. "They shot him in the back," Mary said. "They shot him like a dog."[1] He was lying in a pool of his own blood.

Robert's was the first funeral we went to in Walltown. The Northside Baptist Church, just a few blocks down Berkeley Street, was packed with church folk dressed in black, and young guys from the street, still wearing their white T's and baggy jeans. They'd come to say good-bye to their son, their neighbor, their friend. They'd come, perhaps, to hear a word of hope in the midst of their grief. But the Reverend Brian Irving did not offer many words of comfort—his sermon was a call to action. Violence was claiming the lives of young men from our neighborhood, and we had to do something about it.

I immediately thought of the Christian Peacemaker Teams. Since coming back from Iraq, Leah and I had wanted to reconnect with this church-based organization and its strategy of nonviolent direct action. Maybe this was the time. We could call up CPT's Chicago office, bring in some violence-reduction experts, have training sessions at local churches, and build a movement for nonviolent social change. Before we got home from the funeral, I was making plans for next steps. *But wait*, I thought. *I can't just do this myself. I've got to sell some "indigenous leaders" on the idea.* So I started mentioning CPT to a few folks at church and around the neighborhood. "What you know 'bout C-P-T?" one woman asked me. "That's 'Colored People Time' 'round here." I laughed and tried to explain the other CPT. But Chicago and the strategy of nonviolent direct action seemed a long ways away. Somewhere in my explanation — usually pretty close to the beginning — folks lost interest. CPT just didn't sound like good news.

But Walltown needed some good news. And the next Sunday at St. John's, Reverend Daniels brought it. Our community was hurting, he said. We had watched drugs and gangs take control of our children. Now we were watching our children terrorize the neighbors and kill one another. Brother was killing brother. And as with Abel long ago, Lil' Robert's blood was crying out from the ground (see Genesis 4:10). His blood was crying out to God for justice. The Lord had told Solomon these days would come, Reverend Daniels said — days when there would be "a plague among my people" (2 Chronicles 7:13). But God had also said what we must do. "If my people," he continued, "who are called by my name, will humble themselves and pray and seek my face and turn from their wicked ways, then will I hear from heaven . . . and will heal their land" (verse 14). What Walltown needed more than anything else, Reverend Daniels said, was a praying church. If we would seek God's face, God would hear from heaven and heal our broken community. But we had to get serious about seeking God. Reverend Daniels announced that, beginning the next Saturday, we were going to invite neighbors and other churches to join us for prayer walks in the neighborhood. Meet in the church parking lot at 10 a.m., he said.

I hadn't been able to get anyone interested in a church-based program out of Chicago that could come and help us address neighborhood violence. But that next Saturday, more than sixty people showed up to pray and seek God's face in Walltown. Reverend Hayes split us up into groups of seven or eight, assigned each group to walk certain streets, and gave us our charge: "We're marching like they marched around Jericho, ya'll. Satan's had this neighborhood, but God is going to deliver it. Every step we take, we're claiming territory for the Lord." Then she got us started singing as we set out to our assigned streets:

> We've got the vic'try, hallelujah!
> We've got the vic'try, hallelujah!
> Every knee shall bow,
> Every tongue confess,
> He is Lord! He is Lord!
> Every knee shall bow,
> Every tongue confess,
> He is Lord! Oh, He is Lord!

We sang as we walked, someone new starting another song when we'd finished the first. They were all the songs we sang in church every Sunday. But out here on the streets they sounded a rhythm for our steps and spoke to the conditions we could see around us. If "we've got the vic'try" were true, then we didn't have to fear the violence that seemed to have taken over.

Week after week, we gathered on Saturday morning to repeat that truth that seemed so far from reality. The more we sang, the more we believed we could love those young guys we had been afraid to talk to. When we were in prayer groups and passed guys hanging out on a corner, we started stopping to talk to them. We asked them about their lives and listened to their grief over losing Lil' Robert. One Saturday when Reverend Hayes' group was talking to some guys just down the street from where Robert had been shot, she grabbed the hands of the guys next to her and invited them to bow their heads and pray with her. "I plead the blood of Jesus," she began, gripping their hands as she had gripped mine so many times at the Neighborhood Ministry. They didn't all close their eyes, but they didn't walk away, either.

In her work on a theology of "powers and principalities," Marva Dawn writes that "the language of 'the powers' fell out of use during the time of the Reformation, when various apocalyptic sects made Martin Luther and John Calvin cautious about eschatology."[2] Radical sects who were ready to take up arms to bring in God's kingdom scared the Reformers. So white Protestants for the past five hundred years have been hesitant to name the "powers and principalities" and locate themselves in a cosmic battle against them. When it comes to atonement theories — ways of saying what Jesus was doing when He died and rose again — we prefer to think of Jesus as a substitute for the punishment we deserved rather than a mighty victor over the power of Satan in the world, even though both were standard images throughout the Middle Ages. Sure, we sing, "There is power, power, wonder working power . . . in the precious blood of the Lamb." But what we usually mean is that there is power to forgive our sins, not power to combat the Prince of Darkness in this present evil age. In short, white evangelicalism shies away from the apocalyptic language of cosmic struggle when describing the economic, social, and political relationships we find ourselves in. We worry about a "realized eschatology" that puts too much hope in human ability to change this world. Even as we remind ourselves that Jesus could come back anytime, we know that time of reckoning is yet to come. Like Luther and Calvin before us, we're usually cautious about eschatology.

But just fifteen years before Luther nailed his 95 Theses to the door of the Castle Church at Wittenberg, Christopher Columbus didn't hesitate to connect his recent "discovery" of what we now call the Americas to biblical prophesies about the "last days." In a work that he titled *Book of Prophesies*, Columbus attributed his success in exploration to a guiding light that had driven him since a young age:

> Who doubts that this light was from the Holy Spirit . . . whom with rays of marvelous splendor it consoled . . . with forty-four books of the Old Testament and four Evangelists, with twenty-three epistles of those blessed apostles, encouraging me to proceed, and continuously, without stopping a moment, they encouraged me with great haste.[3]

Columbus went on to explain his desire to proselytize the heathen of the new lands God had shown him while also conscripting their gold to fund the conquest of Jerusalem. Because all the nations of the earth had to hear the gospel before the end could come, Columbus believed that God had ordained and guided his discovery to usher in the "new heavens and new earth" that Isaiah foretold (65:17; 66:22). So it was that the land called America came to be imagined as a "New World." As cultural anthropologist Carol Delaney has written,

> The millennial, apocalyptic scenario that stirred Columbus did not die with him but made the transatlantic crossing with the Puritans who founded the "New Jerusalem" in New England. Through the Puritans these ideas entered into the American mainstream where they have had a powerful grip on American imagination, helping to shape a particular vision of the place of the United States in history and the way Americans understand themselves and their destiny.[4]

In some very real ways, then, we traded the biblical notion of a cosmic spiritual struggle that Jesus has already won on the cross for a secular "realized eschatology" that borrowed Scripture's authority to name America's social project. Here in the "New World," white Europeans established a "City on a Hill." But that project required the genocide of native peoples and the creation of race-based slavery to supply free land and an inexpensive labor force.

So while it may be true that Luther and Calvin shied away from apocalyptic language because of its potential to incite violence in sixteenth-century Europe, the same language was used and abused across the Atlantic to justify the shedding of more blood than the world had ever seen before. It was, significantly, the blood of dark-skinned peoples. While white evangelicalism in America invested itself in the social project of nation building and ignored the biblical language of powers, black Christians could not ignore the apocalyptic hope that Scripture offered them as an oppressed people. The world as they knew it was under the control of Satan, the one who seeks "to steal and kill and destroy" (John 10:10). Black Christians saw that white supremacy was a principality that controlled individuals and institutions. Freedom in Christ meant the hope of freedom from death. To a people whose blood had been shed generation after generation, the image of Jesus' blood shed for them was powerful. So they learned to sing with joy,

> I know it was the blood,
> I know it was the blood,
> I know it was the blood that saved me.
> One day when I was lost
> Jesus died on the cross.
> I know it was the blood that saved me.

No preacher of the black church ever articulated the power of Christ's blood more forcefully than Nat Turner, leader of the 1831 slave revolt in Southampton County, Virginia. After killing fifty-five whites on a march to the county seat of Jerusalem, Turner was apprehended. He testified in his confession,

> For as the blood of Christ had been shed on this earth, and had ascended to heaven for the salvation of sinners, and was now returning to earth again in the form of dew [which Turner had observed on the leaves of corn plants] . . . , it was plain to me that the Savior was about to lay down the yoke he had borne for the sins of men, and the great day of judgment was at hand.[5]

At the end of Turner's confession, his recorder, Thomas Gray, noted the composed deliberateness with which he had recounted his acts of killing. "I looked on him," Gray wrote, "and my blood curdled in my veins."[6] The violence of white supremacy had been turned on its head. While the retaliation that Turner imagined and carried out may have been an anomaly, the revolutionary hope that the blood of Jesus inspired in him was not. For a people beaten and bloodied, there was power in the blood — power to change the world that is into the world that ought to be.

The revolutionary spirit of prophetic black Christianity that is embodied in Nat Turner has scared me speechless on more than one occasion. It is a sign of trust, I suppose, for black folks to let a white man like me see their raw anger. But it's scary. This revolutionary anger cannot be ignored or written off as fanatical. When, as with Turner, it has resulted in violence, the worst that can be said is that black Christians have stooped to employ the weapons of white supremacy. (When Nat Turner broke into the homes of white landowners in Southampton County, he was intentional about shooting them with their own guns.)

But as the apostle Paul said, "we are more than conquerors through him who loved us" (Romans 8:37). The great prophetic tradition of the black church has consistently risen above retaliatory violence to name the principality of white supremacy and insist that it, like all other powers, has been put to death on the cross. All people are set free from its power by the blood of Jesus. When we worship Jesus, my black sisters and brothers say, we participate in that new reality where God "has made the two one and has destroyed the barrier, the dividing wall of hostility" (Ephesians 2:14). So it's possible to go to the streets when the streets become violent and proclaim an end to hostilities in the name of Jesus. It's even possible to invite white folks to walk with you. Because Jesus has broken down the dividing wall, I can learn from Reverend Daniels and Reverend Hayes what it means to plead the blood of Jesus.

In the spring of 2006, after we had been at St. John's for nearly three years, a black female student from the historically black North Carolina Central University accused three young white men from Duke's lacrosse team of raping her. The case became increasingly confused and complicated as the months wore on, and in early 2007, the Attorney General's office dropped charges against the three white students.

However, in the days following the event in the spring of 2006, the case became a media frenzy. Satellite trucks and video cameras from every major news network descended on Duke's campus and the Durham County courthouse. Had these white students from an elite university really raped a black coed from the historically black university across town? The racial divide that we had been trying to navigate for three years was suddenly a national news story.

As it happened, the week this story broke, Reverend William Barber was scheduled to preach in the chapel at Duke Divinity School. Over the years, even after the relationship between Quaker Gap and Greenleaf had faded, Reverend Barber and I had stayed in touch. I'd preached at his church, and he had sent me occasional notes of encouragement. I had called to congratulate him when he was elected president of North Carolina's NAACP chapter. And I had noted that he was scheduled to preach at the Divinity School in April. But no one could have anticipated how sorely we would need a word from Reverend Barber.

Because of his position with the NAACP, Reverend Barber spoke out early about the racially charged rape case, insisting on a fair and thorough legal process for everyone involved. When he came to Duke's chapel on April 4, Reverend Barber came as a preacher in the tradition of prophetic black Christianity. He didn't fail to note that the date, April 4, was the same day Dr. Martin

Luther King Jr. had been assassinated in Memphis, Tennessee, thirty-eight years before. Insisting that we "listen to the prophet," Reverend Barber took on the mantle of the one who had called the church to serve as America's conscience in midst of the Civil Rights Movement. Barber noted that the media was consistently calling the white Duke students "lacrosse players" while identifying the black Central student as an "exotic dancer" or "stripper." Whatever the facts of the case, this woman was a human being, Barber shouted from the pulpit. This case lay open a wound that ran deep in the soul of Durham. And we in the church couldn't act as though that wound didn't touch us.

"There's trouble at the table," Barber said, referring to 1 Corinthians 11. "I hear that when you come together as a church, there are divisions among you" (verse 18). We were a divided church in Durham, not trusting in the blood of Jesus to unify us in love. Reverend Barber called us to lament—to take responsibility for the devastating reality that this case exposed and cry out to God for our salvation. The church couldn't hide behind the walls of a chapel; we had to stand up in public and cry out to God. But if we would confess our sin and stand together before God, there was hope, Barber proclaimed. "Yes, there's trouble at the table, but every day there's something that gives us hope at the table." The blood that reminds us of Christ's death at our hands is the same blood that brings us together. In our deepest tragedy, there is hope. "This has bridged what hundreds of years hasn't been able to bridge," Barber said with a smile. "We're doing something here."

White and black together, we walked out of the chapel onto Duke's main quad, held hands, and prayed. "Forgive us for the divisions we have allowed to exist between us and the community," one local black pastor prayed. "Forgive us for not challenging attitudes of arrogance and pride. Forgive us, Lord, for our culpability."[7] My eyes closed, I listened to the groans of black brothers and sisters who felt the pain that could not be "fixed" by anyone. Their groans made me tremble, and I wanted to speak out against a culture of use and disposal, to at least organize a unified response from the churches. But there was nothing I could do to heal this wound. There was nothing anyone could do.

I opened my eyes and looked around at some of the white administrators who were standing in the circle. In their faces I saw the dread that I could feel in my stomach. It was a mixture of the longing for justice that had been stirred by Reverend Barber's sermon and the realization that there was absolutely nothing we could do. We who were used to fixing problems had little experience crying out to God. Were we just supposed to stand there and wait? I felt myself torn in two — divided between a history that assumed white power and a tradition of prophetic Christianity. Ever since I'd first heard Reverend Barber preach the gospel ten years before, I had been learning to see the world differently. From Stokes County to Philadelphia to Iraq to Walltown and St. John's, I'd chased after Jesus, trying to live in the new world of His kingdom. But here I was at Duke, torn between two ways of seeing the world, not sure what to do.

The next week was Holy Week, and I was scheduled to preach in the chapel from the same pulpit where Reverend Barber had held forth. The text for the day was from John's gospel, chapter 13, where it says that Jesus was troubled and told His disciples, "One of you is going to betray me" (verse 21). I thought about what it must have felt like for Judas to hear Jesus say that. Here was a man who had left everything he had going for him to follow Jesus. He'd made the sacrifice, no doubt, because he believed in the new reality that Jesus was preaching. Judas had believed that the kingdom was going to make a difference in the world. And he had believed in Jesus. But things hadn't unfolded as Judas had hoped. The poor weren't getting fed in great numbers and the prisoners weren't getting set free. The revolution Jesus had promised didn't seem to be panning out. And Judas didn't know what to do. Just like I didn't.

It must have been terrifying, I thought, to hear Jesus say, "One of you is going to betray me." Especially if Judas was already flirting with a plan to take things into his own hands and do something. Even worse to have Jesus give you the bread and the wine, say, "This is My body . . . this is My blood," and then say, "What you are about to do, do quickly" (verse 27). In those two men — Jesus and Judas — I saw embodied the battle that I felt inside of me. On the one hand, the desire to give myself in love and wait on the Lord to do what He'd already said He would do. On the other hand, the desire to do something — and quickly — to fix the racial mess that history had handed us. Judas, I realized, was the white boy in me. There was trouble at the table, and the white boy in me wanted to flee.

I started my sermon for the last week of Lent with a confession: "This is the time when white boys flee," I told the mostly white crowd gathered in the chapel. I admitted I could feel the urge. Like Judas running to the Sanhedrin, part of me wanted to go to the university president's office and demand reform of a campus culture that for decades had taught white students to use and abuse the bodies of black women who cleaned their toilets after drunken parties. We had no way to know whether this particular woman had been raped by the accused lacrosse players, but no one was denying that they had paid money to use her as live pornography. And there wasn't any sense pretending the national media was in town because they cared about the woman. Some white boys who were supposed to be getting educated to run our society had been accused of "going too far" and acting irresponsibly. That's why CNN was there. The white boy in me wanted to run in front of the camera and say exactly what ought to be done to get things back under control.

But Jesus gave His body and His blood to Judas. That's what the text for the day said. Jesus basically was saying, "Do what you have to do, but know this: my blood is for you." I noted what Judas ran to — the Sanhedrin, the place of power. But I also asked the church to pay attention to what Judas ran from: He was fleeing from Jesus' love.

Willard Waller, who studied marriages in the 1930s, developed what he called the "principle of least interest" to describe the relationships he observed. In any relationship, he said, the person who loves the least has the most power. To gain power in a relationship, you have to withhold love. Whoever loves the least is in control. I learned this principle in high school. When someone was leaving messages on my answering machine, I knew I was in charge. I had power in the relationship. But the moment I fell for someone and found myself with sweaty palms trying to dial her number, I knew I'd lost control. Whoever loves the most has the least power.

I told the church that I thought we could choose to see the world from one of two perspectives: from a position of power or from a position of love. We could, with Judas, put our hope in what we could do to overcome the injustice of the world. Or we could, with Jesus, speak the truth and love our enemies to the end. We could assume the position of the white boys, or we could, with Jesus, put ourselves in the place of the black woman, learn to see the world from her perspective, and choose to love our enemies, even if it cost us our lives.

I went on to say that if we want to know what the love of Jesus looks like in America, there are no greater icons than black women. Then I told the story of Annelle Ponder and Fannie Lou Hamer, two black women who were arrested for questioning the white power structure in the 1960s and taken to a jail in Winona, Mississippi. Separated in a different cell, Ms. Hamer heard Ms. Ponder's body hit the concrete floor of the jailhouse. She listened to her friend scream as she was beaten by police officers. "She kept screamin'," Ms. Hamer said, "and they kept beatin' her, and finally she started prayin' for 'em, and she asked God to have mercy on 'em because they didn't know what they was doin'." When they got to Ms. Hamer's cell, the white jailer called in two black men to beat her body until it was, as she later said, "hard as a bone." Later, when Ms. Hamer was escorted by the jailer to her trial, she asked him, "Do you people ever think or wonder how you'll feel when the time comes you'll have to meet God?" By some miracle, after suffering the hell of human betrayal at its worst, Ms. Hamer was concerned about the fate of this white man's soul. "It wouldn't solve any problem for me to hate whites just because they hate me," she said. "Oh, there's so much hate, only God has kept us Negroes sane."[8]

If we want to know what it means to be Christian in America, we have to look to Ms. Hamer and Ms. Ponder. They are the embodiment of a prophetic Christianity that names and engages the principalities in the power of Jesus' blood. Determined that segregation was a dehumanizing evil that resulted from the principality of white supremacy, they stood up in the "somebody-ness" that the gospel made possible and said that segregation had to go. But when their bodies were nearly beaten to death by defenders of segregation, these women loved their enemies and prayed for those who were persecuting them. In doing so, they exemplified the double miracle of the black church in America. The first miracle is that a people torn from their homes and brutally enslaved in a land not their own would learn the gospel from their white oppressors and hear it as good news. But the second miracle is even more profound: that after centuries of oppression and disenfranchisement at the hands of white folks, black Christians would pray for us, love us, and invite us to come and learn from them what it means to plead the blood of Jesus. There are some things that nobody but God can do.

"The church must be the place in which white supremacy is analyzed and deconstructed," writes Eugene Rivers, pastor of the Azusa Christian Community. "For those of us who love the church, this is redemptive. . . . The church has been no less divided about white supremacist ideology than society. The blood of Christ was not heavy enough, not deep enough, to bridge the chasm as the ideology developed."[9] This is the stark reality of the church's history in America. White supremacy has been more determinative than the blood of Jesus in shaping our worship, our readings of Scripture, our economic relationships, our political affiliations, our notions of what is beautiful, even our preferences in entertainment. The abolition of slavery did not fix this disorder. The Civil Rights Movement did not either. Desegregation, affirmative action, and multicultural education together have not been able to challenge the power of race. As my teacher Willie Jennings used to say, "The only force in the modern world that ever challenged the power of race was the evangelical conversion experience." What he meant was that the only time the church as a social reality has ever lived an alternative to the white supremacy of our society was when white and black together got "struck dead" by Jesus and woke up to find themselves as brothers and sisters, "washed . . . in the blood of the Lamb" (Revelation 7:14).

To plead the blood of Jesus in our racialized society is to confess that white Christians like me need to learn from the black church's prophetic tradition of apocalyptic hope and radical love what it means to be the church. We need to be struck dead in the social space that black folks own and wake up to find ourselves under the leadership of folks like Ms. Hamer and Ms. Ponder, Reverend Hayes and Reverend Daniels. Only they can teach us what it means to be the church in America. Only with them can we become the body of Christ.

In his letter to the Ephesians, Paul says that Jesus came to "preach peace to you who were far away and peace to those who were near" (2:17). It's kind of Paul to say "those who were near" instead of "us who were near." But "us" is what he means, because Paul was a Jew. He was a member of the people who had been chosen by God, the people who had received the gift of God's Law, the people through whom God had promised to save the whole world. Our friend Ched Myers likes to say that Paul's letter to the Ephesians is the Jewish "Letter from a Birmingham Jail" because in it Paul (a member of the persecuted minority) makes an appeal to Gentiles (the powerful enemies of his people) to believe on Jesus and join the family of God. That's a lot like what Martin Luther King Jr. was doing in Birmingham: calling on the white ministers who had benefited from segregation to join the black Civil Rights Movement and be part of the beloved community that Jesus had made possible.

"You were dead in your transgressions and sins, in which you used to live when you followed the ways of this world and of the ruler of the kingdom of the air," Paul says to the Gentiles (2:1-2). White supremacy is a principality that shapes how we live and makes our lives a living death. We have, for centuries, been held captive within the logic of race by the ruler of the kingdom of the air. "Because of his great love for us, God, who is rich in mercy, made us alive with Christ even when we were dead in transgressions" (verses 4-5). Even while we were enjoying our "freedom" to buy and consume and amuse ourselves to death, God entrusted the prophetic gospel of apocalyptic hope and radical love to a black church that survived on the underside of the American dream. Then in His mercy, God invited those of us who were far away to believe that good news and become part of His family: "It is by grace you have been saved, through faith—and this not from yourselves, it is the gift of God—not by works, so that no one can boast. For we are God's workmanship, created in Christ Jesus to do good works, which God prepared in advance for us to do" (verses 8-10).

Paul insists that the Ephesians remember how they had been outsiders, excluded from God's promise, "without hope and without God in the world" (verse 12). We can't forget that white power is a dead-end enterprise. We can't forget the Judas within us who always "wants what he wants when he wants it" and is willing to get it by whatever means necessary. We can't forget that the assumption of power over and against love is inscribed in the identity of whiteness. "Now in Christ Jesus you who once were far away have been brought near through the blood of Christ. For he himself is our peace, who has made the two one and has destroyed the barrier, the dividing wall of hostility" (verses 13-14). The blood of Jesus is what brings us near. It's the blood that makes it possible for white Christians to stop worshipping white power and learn from those who have known the fellowship of Christ's sufferings. It's the blood that destroys the racial barriers that divide a town like Durham. It's the blood that breaks down the hostility that would keep me from wanting to join a black church and keep a black church from wanting to welcome me.

Jesus had made reconciliation possible through His blood.

"His purpose was to create in himself one new man out of the two, thus making peace, and in this one body to reconcile both of them to God through the cross, by which he put to death their hostility" (verses 15-16). Out of two peoples, God has made one new body. Black and white together, the blood of Jesus runs through our veins. As this reconciled community, Ephesians says, we are reconciled to God through the Cross. This is what salvation means. Like we sing at St. John's, "I know it was the blood that saved me."

In his book *Will the Circle Be Unbroken?* radio personality Studs Terkel published his interview with Mamie Mobley, the mother of Emmett Till, who was killed in Mississippi by two white men in 1955. Till's killers were acquitted by an all-white jury, and the case gained international attention, becoming a significant prelude to the Civil Rights Movement. When Terkel interviewed Mobley in 2000, she recalled what it was like for her to see her son's mutilated body.

"I had ordered Emmett's body brought back to Chicago," she said. "It was in three boxes. . . . Each had the Mississippi seal and a padlock on it." Mobley said she wanted to verify that it was her son's body in the box and not dirt or cement, so she requested a hammer to break the locks. When they finally got through the boxes to the body bag, the undertaker unzipped the bag and Mobley saw her son's body, covered in lime. "They hosed him down. And, oh, my God, I knew what the odor was by then. It was not the lime, that was my son I was smelling."[10]

Mobley described the horrific experience of examining her son's mutilated body, beginning at his feet and naming each body part in a litany of horror. She said that when she got to his head, "There was no ear. It was gone. I was looking up the side of his face and I could see daylight on the other side. I said, 'Oh, my God!' The tears were falling, and I was brushing tears away because I had to see."[11] I've never read a more disturbing account of brutality than Mobley's remembrance of her son's mutilated body. The first time I ever read it, I wished that Terkel had not asked her to relive the nightmare. But then I got to the end. After recalling the whole incident, Mobely shared with Terkel what theological sense she'd made of the hell she had been through. Mobley says better than I ever could what it means for white folks like me to learn from the black church that we have been saved by the blood of Jesus:

> Later I was reading the Scriptures, and it told how
> Jesus had been led from judgment hall to judgment
> hall all night long, how He had been beaten — and so
> much that no man would ever sustain the horror of his
> beating, that His face was just in ribbons. And I thought
> about it, and I said, "Lord, do you mean to tell me that
> Emmett's beating did not equal the one that was given
> to Jesus?" And I said, "My God, what Jesus must have
> suffered."
>
> And then I thought about some of the pictures we
> see, where He has this neat little crown of thorns and
> you see a few rivulets of blood coming down, but His
> face is intact. And according to Scripture, that is not
> true. His visage was scarred more than any other man's
> had ever been or will be.
>
> And that's when I really was able to assess what Jesus
> had given for us, the love He had for us.
>
> And I saw Emmett and his scars. Lord, I saw the
> stigmata of Jesus. The spirit spoke to me as plainly as

I'm talking to you now. Jesus had come and died that we might have a right to eternal life or eternal hell and damnation. Emmett had died that men might have freedom here on earth. . . . If Jesus Christ died for our sins, Emmett Till bore our prejudices.[12]

BLESSED BE THE TIE THAT BINDS

On the one side of the racial divide you have a church tied to the dictates of survival and on the other side is a church tied to the power of whiteness. And in both cases the church gives no freedom; its mission, its purpose, its very being is inscribed within a racial logic that refuses to yield. Yet the question remains . . . What of our freedom in Christ, our freedom from the powers?

Willie Jennings

SEVEN

Climbing Jacob's Ladder

Sometime when I was in college, I stopped getting dressed up for church. I think it was a gradual process, like the addition of the proverbial "freshman fifteen" that so many college students experience, only mine was a gradual process of subtraction. I lost the tie that I'd been taught to wear on special occasions like Easter and Christmas. My "Sunday shoes"—the kind you have to polish—wore out, and I didn't bother replacing them. I remembered a fellow named John from back in King, North Carolina, who wore the same work pants and button-up shirt every day of his life, no matter what he was doing. I'd seen him wear that uniform at church, and I'd seen him wear it when he mowed his yard. This had meant next to nothing to me when I was growing up. But as I was trying to sort through what it meant to be an authentic, everyday follower of Jesus, I for some reason remembered John and more or less assumed his uniform as my own.

As I look back on it, I think my questions about how to dress came out of the conversations I had with homeless folks in Center City, Philadelphia. On park benches and in subway stations I got to know people like Pops and Edward and Anthony who wore the same clothes every day. When we talked, they often smelled bad. But those guys became my teachers. The more I got to know them, the more I thought about them at church on Sunday mornings. We were spiritually connected. But as I listened to the gospel readings with them in mind, I heard the Bible talking about things as practical as food and clothing: "The man with two tunics should share with him who has none, and the one who has food should do the same" (Luke 3:11). I didn't have a tunic, but I had some extra shirts and hats and socks—not to mention access to more food than I could eat. When I met people who needed them, I started giving some of my clothes away. What I kept were a few pairs of work pants and some long-sleeve shirts. And I wore them everywhere I went—even to church.

The exception to my rule was weddings and funerals. I bought a black suit to get married in, and I put it on again to preach my great-granny's funeral. Maybe it was just the romantic in me, but I figured celebrations of life and love just weren't the times to question social norms, which is why when we started going to St. John's, I still had a black suit in my closet. And since it was strange enough that we weren't from Walltown and our skin was white, I decided I'd wear the suit to worship service. After all, everyone at St. John's got dressed up for worship, from the children in Sunday school to the mothers of the church decked out in white suits and white hats with white lace on the trim. Most of the white churches I'd gone to since leaving King had been pretty casual about dress anyway. What you wore just didn't seem to matter. But proper dress clearly mattered at St. John's. People worked hard to look good for church.

I came to St. John's to learn, so I tried to understand what getting dressed up for church meant to folks. Clearly, everyone in the congregation had relationships with people like the guys I'd known on the streets in Philadelphia. Those guys were their cousins and uncles and sometimes their sons. In more than one case, I learned, the man who put a suit on to come to St. John's on Sunday morning had been on the streets himself—and not so long ago. But church for him was a different reality than the street. While the street had been a place of bondage and addiction, the church was a place of freedom. God had saved him from life on the street and given him new life at St. John's. Conversion didn't just feel different—it looked different. You could see it in the way the man dressed.

As I got to know people at St. John's, I learned that you don't have to have lived on the streets to know the harsh economic realities that people who end up there can tell you about. To be black in America is to be told ten thousand times a day that you live in a world you do not own. This is why the church has been such an important center for black community life in America. Here is a space that black folks have owned, even when master or the bank owned the building, since before emancipation. Here black women and men have held positions of authority, instructed their own children, mourned their dead, and, most importantly, proclaimed the word of God Almighty. In a world where black bodies have been owned and objectified, used and abused, the black church has been the one place of retreat where dignity could be restored to the bodies and souls of black folk.

A white guy like me can't ignore that history when trying to understand why black folks get dressed up to go to church. But to look just at the history would be to overlook what every black person I've ever talked to actually says about dressing up for church: namely, that they do it out of reverence for Christ. You put on your best clothes to go to church because church is God's house, they say. And God's house ain't like Uncle Leroy's house. God's house is holy. God's house is where the omnipresent Lord has requested that we come into His presence with thanksgiving and enter His courts with praise. Out of respect and honor for God, we come to church dressed in our very best. That's what folks at St. John's say. Their reasons are not just historical — they're theological.

How's a twentysomething white guy going to argue with that? As I listened to folks at St. John's, I started thinking that my convictions about uniform dress from college days had been more than a little reactionary, probably the result of trying to think through big social issues like poverty and homelessness while spending most of my time on a college campus where my meals were prepared, my toilet cleaned, my halls swept by mostly black and Latino workers whom I'd never gotten to know. What did they care if I'd decided to stop dressing up for church? It sure didn't do them any good. So when I was visiting my parents' house, I searched in the back of a closet and found the old suit I'd worn when I worked as a page in the Senate. The next Sunday I mixed the olive blazer from that suit with the black pants from my other and put on a pair of shiny black shoes. "All right!" brother Desi hollered at me when I walked into the church. "Brother Jonathan's got it goin' on today!"

Not having spent any money to put together my little Sunday wardrobe, I felt pretty good about it for a few weeks. Then one evening, as I was leaving the Neighborhood Ministry office over on Knox Street, I saw William pushing his bicycle down the street. He flashed his signature smile — humble, with squinty eyes and dimples in his cheeks. I'd met William on the street at some point and knew that he was the "Bike Man." Anything wrong with a bike, William could fix it. We often had conversations on the sidewalk. But I also knew that William was an alcoholic. He knew it too and had told me on more than one occasion that he wanted help. I asked him how he was doing that night outside the Ministry office. "I need some help," he said. "I've got to change some things in my life." We talked about God's power to change things — things we know that we can't change ourselves. I asked William if he would come to church with me on Sunday. "Oh, I couldn't," he said, looking down at the ground. "I don't have any clothes to wear."

"William," I said, "God loves you. He doesn't care what you're wearing. Come in whatever you've got."

"God might not care, but the people at church do." He said it, and I knew it was true. Nobody would believe that William had changed until he came to church with a new suit on. But William knew that he needed to change. And he needed help to do it. Grace was being offered at God's house on Sunday morning, but William didn't feel he could go there until he got cleaned up and found some church clothes. When I went to decide which of my two suits I was going to wear the next Sunday morning, I thought of William and chose neither.

But I did wear the nicest-looking work pants I had. I wore them because I felt torn. I could understand the historical and theological reasons why folks would dress up for worship at St. John's, but I could also see the barrier it was creating for someone who desperately needed the church. What was I supposed to do? The questions made me feel lonely, and I didn't know how to talk about it. Then one Sunday, as we were leaving Sunday school class, Reverend Daniels asked me if I thought I had a word I could preach that morning. He'd had a hard week and was beginning to feel sick. Could I fill in as preacher? It just so happened that I was preaching that evening at another church and had already prepared a sermon for that service. With a few modifications, I could preach it at St. John's. "But I'll have to go home and change," I said, feeling awkward in my work pants and tennis shoes. "No, that's all right," Reverend Daniels said. "This is dress-down Sunday. It'll be good for the preacher to dress down too."

Listening to Reverend Daniels over the next few months, I realized I wasn't alone in my questions about how we dress as a church and what it communicates. In conversations, Reverend Daniels shared about his desire for the church to be welcoming to anyone, especially those who felt left out and excluded. He preached more than once about how some of us were so proud of what we were wearing that we didn't have time to think about God or our neighbor. He hammed it up a little bit, strutting across the stage and impersonating church folk in their finest clothes. A few Sundays he even left his suit and tie at home, preaching the sermon with his shirttail hanging out.

I was relieved to learn that even traditions that existed for good reasons could be questioned and modified. I wasn't alone in struggling with something as simple as how to dress. St. John's represented a living tradition, which meant that things were always changing and people were always talking about what needed to change and why. If we were really going to be a part of this church, we had to learn how to participate in that conversation. My struggle with dress was not my own but one I had to share with a body of people who wanted to follow Jesus together in Walltown. That might mean looking like a fool sometimes — or, even worse, a racist. But to be real it would have to be honest, for as we love to say at St. John's, "God is spirit, and his worshipers must worship in spirit and in truth" (John 4:24).

Living traditions, like families, are messy. Scholars can analyze history and point to ideal types that represent the different strands of a tradition. But traditions are made up of people like you and me who not only regularly contradict our highest ideals in practice but also frequently find ourselves believing things we thought we had definitively rejected. At the heart of the black church tradition, there is a prophetic faith of apocalyptic hope and radical love. But that doesn't mean prophetic faith is the only strand in the black church tradition or that any church lives it faithfully all the time. No community is untouched by the sin that twists human desires and the powers that offer themselves as false gods to be worshipped.

The same ideology of white power that shaped white Christianity also influenced the formation of the black church. If white Christians had submitted themselves more to Jesus than to the idol of whiteness, they would have embraced black brothers and sisters as equals and there would never have been a "white church." But there would not have been a black church either. All of our histories have been compromised by the sin of white supremacy.

In his classic text *The Souls of Black Folk*, W.E.B. DuBois wrote that "by the middle of the eighteenth century the black slave had sunk, with hushed murmurs, to his place at the bottom of a new economic system, and was unconsciously ripe for a new philosophy of life. Nothing suited his condition then better than the doctrines of passive submission embodied in the newly learned Christianity."[1] DuBois believed that this strand of "weak Christianity" made black folk into kowtowing "Uncle Toms" who willingly suffered whatever the white establishment imposed upon them while putting their hope in the heaven that a white god promised when they finished living through hell on earth.

This "religious fatalism" not only led black folk to participate in their own oppression, DuBois argued, over time it also muted the moral significance of their actions. So weak Christianity was to blame for marital infidelity, habits of deception, and a culture of crime. If this world was not home, DuBois said, people ended up doing whatever they felt like doing.

On the other hand, DuBois also saw a strand of religious radicalism in the black church tradition. Just as Nat Turner had found in Scripture an apocalyptic vision that inspired revolt, many black Christians in the antebellum South had learned to sing,

Before I'll be a slave
I'll be buried in my grave
And go home to my Lord
And be free.

As a sociologist and historian, DuBois could see how this strand of the tradition had contributed to the abolition movement in the early and mid-nineteenth century. So while there was a "weak Christianity" that DuBois despised, there was also this strand of apocalyptic revolutionary Christianity that had anticipated the end of slavery as the very coming of the Lord. Looking critically at this strand some forty years after emancipation, however, DuBois complained that "every tendency is to excess — radical complaint, radical remedies, bitter denunciation or angry silence. . . . [Northern radicals] despise the submission and subservience of Southern Negroes, but offer no other means by which a poor and oppressed minority can exist side by side with its masters."[2] Having achieved the freedom that it longed for, this revolutionary strand of the black church tradition didn't offer a plan for how to achieve a new world where black and white could live together.

So at the beginning of the twentieth century, DuBois looked at the black church and saw it divided between "hypocritical compromise" and "radicalism," neither of which seemed very hopeful. On the one hand, there was a strand of the tradition that encouraged patient, quiet, and submissive work within the world that white power had created. Black women and men could work, beg, and borrow (and steal when nobody was looking) until they got enough money together to buy some land and send their kids to college, thus carving out a space to survive in a world that was not their own. "Is this not . . . the only method by which undeveloped races have gained the right to share modern culture?" DuBois asked. Maybe so, but he was not satisfied with the assumptions of such a history. "The price of culture is a Lie."[3] On the other hand, though, those who raged against the Lie of a society that systematically excluded blacks had no way of achieving the new world they dreamed of. The radical strand of the black church tradition continued to offer a critical edge, but DuBois could see that criticism spiraling into cynicism and self-destruction long before anyone had ever heard of "black power."

Despite his bleak analysis of the black church tradition, DuBois nevertheless knew that the black community needed a religious vision to move forward. "Back of this still broods silently the deep religious feeling of the real Negro heart, the stirring, unguided might of powerful human souls who have lost the guiding star of the past and are seeking in the great night a new religious ideal."[4] DuBois believed that this religious vision was, more than anything else, what black folk had to offer America. That's why he wrote about the souls of black folks. In many ways his whole life was an attempt to articulate a new religious ideal for the black community.

Fifty years after he'd graduated from college, DuBois returned to his alma mater, Fisk University, to deliver the commencement address. There he proclaimed his vision for the church, insisting that "the function of the Negro church . . . has got to be brought back, or shall we say forward, to the simple duty of teaching ethics."[5] He spoke as a seer about his vision for

> a church with a cooperative store in the Sunday school room; with physician, dentist, nurse, and lawyer to help, serve, and defend the congregation; with library, nursery school, and a regular succession of paid and trained lecturers and discussion; they had radio and moving pictures and out beyond the city a farm with house and lake. They had a credit union, group insurance and building and loan association. The members paid for this not by contributions but by ten dollars a month each of regular dues and those who would join this church must do more than profess to love God.[6]

Refusing both Uncle Tom's subservience and Nat Turner's radicalism, DuBois dreamed of a church that would serve as economic, social, and political center for a strong black community. Here black women and men would create the world they longed to see while at the same time advocating for social change that would transform the racist systems around them. In many ways, DuBois was imagining the church that would emerge in the Civil Rights Movement to draw on the best of the tradition and put faith to work in society. He dreamed of a church that would actually make a difference in a world where black folks get crushed and forgotten.

The first summer we lived in Walltown, Bahari J. Harris proposed a partnership between St. John's and The Navigators to run a summer camp for teenagers in the neighborhood. Bahari worked for The Navigators, an international parachurch organization that focuses on Christian discipleship. Though The Navigators had worked on military bases and college campuses for most of their history, they sent Bahari, a gifted black graduate of one of their college chapters, to Durham to be part of their new "urban huddle" there. His job was to try to figure out how The Navigators could partner with local churches to do urban ministry.

Bahari looked around Durham and saw how black kids were slipping through the cracks. Though their grandmothers brought them to church from the time they were born, they stopped coming about the time they hit their teens. The churches didn't know how to reach them, the school system was failing them, and most of them came from single-parent homes. So the girls were getting pregnant and the guys were getting guns to prove they were tough enough to run with a gang. Those who didn't end up dead like Lil' Robert in Walltown were on track to land in prison before they were twenty-one. Bahari looked at these kids and knew that God wanted him to offer them some hope, so he came to St. John's with the idea of a summer camp.

"Durham has summer programs for young kids," Bahari said, "but we're losing the older ones to the gangs. Let's start a camp for teenagers where they can get four things: spiritual development, recreation, financial literacy, and entrepreneurship training." Bahari said that The Navigators could bring camp counselors in from their college ministries if St. John's would help recruit the kids and provide a space to host the camp. Kids who participated in the program would work through a Job Club with local businesses and start college funds with the money they earned. For six weeks in the summer, teenagers from Walltown would have a chance to build healthy community, imagine new possibilities for their lives, make some money, and have some fun. Here was Christianity that made a difference. Bahari even had a name for it: Urban Hope.

When all the logistics were figured out for that first summer, Bahari and the church asked me to work as a counselor for Urban Hope. So I was up every morning and ready to go by seven, leading Bible studies and organizing a basketball league, getting to know the kids in our neighborhood and inviting them to dream bigger dreams. "We've got to show these kids that Jesus is real, ya'll," Bahari would say. "The church hasn't been relevant in their lives." He sounded like W.E.B. DuBois, and he was right: The power of the gospel didn't mean anything if it couldn't confront the powers of racism, poverty, violence, and abuse in real lives. The church was irrelevant unless it could offer these kids a way out of the hell they were living in.

So we talked a lot in our counselor meetings about empowerment. How does God reach a kid whose spirit has been crushed and let her know He loves her? How do we lift up kids who've been told that they're not important and help them imagine a different future? What hope does the gospel offer? What would a good life look like in Walltown?

We put together Bible studies to teach the kids not only how much God loved them but also how God was able to "make a way out of no way." Then we designed rap sessions where we invited kids to share their feelings, talk about their dreams, and imagine what life could look like for them. It took a while to get the kids talking, but when they did they had a lot to say. They felt bitterness about other people having stuff while they had next to nothing. They dreamed about living like rap stars and professional athletes in big houses, driving fancy cars, spending money, and having sex. They could imagine, for the most part, little more than what they had seen on TV. We'd asked them to be honest with us, but their dreams were almost as scary as their reality. What if empowerment ended up meaning that black folks had just as much a right to live reckless and excessive lives as white folks?

We were ready, as DuBois had been a century before, to point out how freedom can be abused. We had honest talks about budgeting and financial responsibility, sexually transmitted diseases, and family values. We even got the kids to dress up in professional clothing and present business plans to their parents and other members of the community. In six short weeks they'd made great strides toward being responsible citizens. But the question about what we were empowering them for lingered. Maybe they were more responsible, but were they any closer to the way of Jesus?

I didn't want my question to sound like a criticism of Urban Hope. What The Navigators and St. John's were doing together was a huge step in the right direction. In Walltown the church was doing something about the problems that people usually just complained about. We weren't preaching pie-in-the-sky-by-and-by and we weren't abandoning kids to the angry violence of the gangs. Urban Hope was building a new kind of community for a new generation in Walltown. But we were, at the same time, caught up in a history that was bigger than us. Somehow, even when we started with Bible study, it was easier to make young people into good citizens than it was to make them into good disciples. The American dream felt more powerful than the call to take up a cross and follow Jesus. Given the opportunity, these kids wanted to climb the ladder. But it wasn't Jacob's ladder, the one we sing about at church where "every round goes higher, higher" toward the kingdom of God; it was the social ladder of American capitalism where going up means getting yours in a dog-eat-dog world.

In Mark's gospel, after Jesus drives the money changers out of the temple and debates all the major interpreters of Israel's tradition, the scribes send their sharpest scholar to ask Jesus one last question: "Of all the commandments, which is the most important?" (Mark 12:28). Jesus answers with the Shema. It's like quoting the Lord's Prayer at a seminary. Jesus rattles off a commandment that the scribe and everyone else who is listening have memorized and say every day: "Hear, O Israel, the Lord our God, the Lord is one. Love the Lord your God with all your heart and with all your soul and with all your mind and with all your strength" (verses 29-30). And then, without missing a beat, Jesus tacks on a teaching from Leviticus 19:18: "The second is this: 'Love your neighbor as yourself.' There is no commandment greater than these" (verse 31). Jesus takes this quote from a part of Leviticus where the people of God are reminded of their obligation to take care of the poor and the strangers in their land. He says that this social vision is inseparable from true worship. You can't say that you love God and not love your neighbor. A church that doesn't make a difference in the real world is no church at all.

Mark says that when the scribe heard it, he replied, "Well said, teacher" (verse 32). This scholar listens to Jesus' interpretation of the law, sees how He pieces the Shema together with the command to be merciful, and says, indeed, love of God and neighbor is what it's all about. That is the heart of the law—to refuse the distinction between faith and politics and insist that true religion is about a vision for how we live together. The scholar could just as well have been W.E.B. DuBois himself. "The function of the Negro church, instead of being that of building edifices, paying old debts, holding revivals, and staging entertainments, has got to be brought back, or shall we say forward, to the simple duty of teaching ethics."[7] Loving God is about more than playing church; it means loving your neighbor as yourself.

But when Jesus hears the scribe agree with Him, He says to him, "You are not far from the kingdom of God" (verse 34). Not far, but not quite there. Something is still missing. I've thought a lot about what Jesus meant by that. What was the scribe missing? Mark says that after Jesus told him he wasn't far from the kingdom of God, no one dared ask Jesus any more questions. And I guess I can understand why. Because it's hard to hear that you got close but just missed the most important thing in the world. My hunch is that it was hard for Jesus to say it too. Hard, but necessary, because Jesus loved the scribe, just like He loved the rich young ruler who, in Mark's words, "went away sad, because he had great wealth" (10:22). Jesus loved him enough that He didn't want him to walk away thinking he understood the kingdom when he didn't. Jesus didn't want this learned scholar to miss the most important thing because in all his learning he had misunderstood what God's kingdom was about, so Jesus asked him a question:

> "How is it that the teachers of the law say that the Christ is the son of David? David himself, speaking by the Holy Spirit, declared:
>
> > "'The Lord said to my Lord:
> > "Sit at my right hand
> > until I put your enemies
> > under your feet.'"
>
> David himself calls him 'Lord.' How then can he be his son?" (12:35-37).

If Jesus appeared harsh before, it almost looks like He's making fun of this scholar now. You say the Messiah is to be the son of David, Jesus says. But David called the Messiah his Lord. So which is it? Does the Messiah come before or after David? Jesus seems to say before, suggesting that the Messiah has authority over even David's kingdom. But this isn't just a technical argument about who's in charge of the kingdom; Jesus is trying to make clear what kind of kingdom God wants to bring, because not all kingdoms are created equal. It's not enough to see that Jesus the Messiah has a social vision for a kingdom. Jesus says that God's kingdom doesn't work like David's kingdom. Ultimately, God meant to show in Jesus that He had a different way of ruling the world.

A couple of chapters earlier, speaking to His disciples, Jesus tried to explain it like this:

> You know those that are regarded as rulers of the Gentiles lord it over them, and their high officials exercise authority over them. Not so with you. Instead, whoever wants to become great among you must be your servant, and whoever wants to be first must be slave of all. For even the Son of Man did not come to be served, but to serve, and to give his life as a ransom for many. (Mark 10:42-45)

Jesus wasn't going to be a king like David had been king. Sure, David had been a good king. Jesus wasn't arguing with that. But there was something fundamentally wrong with the way kings ruled before Jesus. The whole order of things had to change, Jesus said—even how people thought about greatness. Jesus didn't come to fulfill the hopes and dreams of a broken world. Jesus came to make possible a new world where we learn together with friends and enemies what it means to hope and dream of a life where we serve one another in God.

I love how I've learned to sing it at St. John's: "We are climbing Jacob's ladder, soldiers of the cross." God invites us to be part of a kingdom, and we're enlisted in an army, for sure. We are at war. With Jesus we wrestle the wild beast of racism in the wilderness of America, but we do not fight like every other kingdom fights. As Paul says in Ephesians, "our struggle is not against flesh and blood, but against the rulers, against the authorities, against the powers of this dark world and against the spiritual forces of evil in the heavenly realms" (6:12). We don't fight like others fight because God has shown us what we're really fighting against. And Jesus has already defeated our real enemy through the Cross. "Having disarmed the powers and authorities, he made a public spectacle of them, triumphing over them by the cross" (Colossians 2:15). That's why we're soldiers of the cross. We struggle in this world as Jesus taught us to struggle — by taking up our cross. We aspire to be as great as Jesus, but great in the same way, which means we aspire to die — and in dying, to discover a new way of life.

In his literary masterpiece *Invisible Man*, Ralph Ellison tells the story of a black man from the Deep South who tries to climb the ladder in America by every means available. He goes off to college, goes north in search of freedom, goes to work for the Communist party on behalf of his people. But in the end he concludes that he is damned by the powers that be in America to be invisible. Though the black church is not considered as a real alternative in Ellison's novel, the two strands of the black church tradition that DuBois identified are carried to their furthest extreme at the end of the story. Ellison's unnamed protagonist is confused for a preacher named Rinehart who, it turns out, makes use of his invisibility to lead a double life. He's a preacher and a pimp at the same time, the extreme of what DuBois called the hypocritical strand of black Christianity. But to a man whose options have been exhausted, Rinehart seems like a real option. Maybe this is the only way to survive in a world that makes you feel invisible.

Ultimately, though, Ellison's protagonist comes to the end of the way of Rinehart because he is recognized as a Communist spokesman and gets caught up in a race riot in Harlem. Following Ras the Destroyer, an apocalyptic figure doing battle on horseback, black folks are looting the white-owned businesses of Harlem and burn down a dilapidated tenement. Ellison follows the radical strand of the black church tradition out to its bitter end in a picture of Harlem burning and white folks hanging in effigy.

But Ellison, like DuBois, saw that neither of these strands offered the prospect of a new reality. "Step outside the narrow borders of reality," he wrote, "and you step into chaos — ask Rinehart, he's a master of it — or imagination."[8] The image Ellison offers for a third way is an image of death. Running away from the race riot, his protagonist falls through a manhole onto a pile of dark coal. He goes underground. He is buried. But there beneath the surface, dead to the world, he begins to imagine new possibilities. "I must shake off the old skin and come up for breath," he says. What follows, I believe, could just as well have run through Jesus' mind in the last moments before His resurrection.

> There's a stench in the air, which, from this distance underground, might be the smell either of death or of spring — I hope of spring. But don't let me trick you, there is a death in the smell of spring and in the smell of thee as in the smell of me.[9]

Ellison saw how easily we are all tricked. The only reality we know is the racialized world of white and black. For white folks it means we think we have to choose — white church or black church? For black folks it also means an either/or — hypocrisy or revolt? Like DuBois we might reject both options and try to forge a third way. But history teaches us, Ellison says, how futile that pursuit has been. "One of the greatest jokes in the world is the spectacle of the whites busy escaping blackness and becoming blacker every day, and the blacks striving toward whiteness, becoming quite dull and gray. None of us seems to know who he is or where he's going."[10] We're confused about our identity and our ultimate goal. We don't know who we are or where we're going. The trick is that we don't recognize how "there is a death in the smell of spring and in the smell of thee as in the smell of me." We don't want to admit that all of us stink of death, but, even more, we can't imagine how death opens the way to a new reality. To step out of the only reality we've known means chaos — or imagination. But in our attempts to avoid the first, we miss even the possibility of the second. What if Jesus died to give us a new identity? What if He rose again to lead us into a world we can't imagine?

Since that first summer of Urban Hope, I've watched a couple of kids from Walltown join the church at St. John's. They come forward at an altar call, make Jesus their choice, and go through "New Members Class" with Sister Parker. The Sunday after they finish their class, the whole church gathers in the basement and sings "Take Me to the Waters" as the candidates for membership line up beside the baptistery, dressed in white robes. Their families are always there, dressed in their Sunday best. Sister Parker pauses to take their picture. But then, one by one, they go down into the waters to be baptized in the name of the Father, and of the Son, and of the Holy Ghost. When the kids come out of the waters, they are members of the church. Somehow, they've been made part of Christ's body.

I don't understand just how all of that works, but I do know that what the church is up to when we baptize those kids is giving them a new identity. We tell them who they are and where they're going. Quoting Paul we say, "I have been crucified with Christ and I no longer live, but Christ lives in me" (Galatians 2:20). To be baptized is to be put to death. If baptism means anything, it means that I'm no longer white because of what Christ did on the cross. And it means that the kids who go down into the waters in the basement of St. John's aren't black anymore when they come up. We've all been crucified with Christ. We don't live anymore, but Christ lives within us.

Acknowledging the stench of death on all of us helps us let go of the identities we thought so important. We were dying, killing ourselves in pursuit of the options that this broken world offered us. I came to St. John's thinking that I had to become black—and maybe I have in some ways. But it's not enough to just become black, because Christ has set us free from the racialized reality of this world. At St. John's we are free to be bound to one another as the people of God. This is who we are.

And where are we going? We are climbing Jacob's ladder. Every round goes higher, higher as we go down the way of the cross, serving one another in the power of God's self-giving love. We are ascending toward greatness by washing one another's feet. Most of this takes place beneath the radar, underground. We struggle to keep a summer camp going and keep peace with one another. We are the church invisible—ignored like Ellison's "invisible man"—finding our identity in the crucified flesh of Jesus. It is Holy Saturday, and we are with Christ in the tomb.

We cannot deny it—the stench of death is all around us. But we know who we are and where we're going. We've heard news of a dead man walking, even climbing Jacob's ladder. Close on his heels we follow, learning what it means to climb up by going down. We are—and are becoming—soldiers of the cross.

EIGHT

The Whole World in His Hands

Whenever Reverend Daniels wants to convince St. John's to do something, he reminds us in his sermon how Jesus said, "If anyone would come after me, he must deny himself and take up his cross and follow me" (Matthew 16:24). Whether he's rallying the troops to petition city hall for a neighborhood recreation center or drafting folks to get up early Sunday morning and cook for homecoming dinner, Reverend Daniels reminds us that Jesus said that Christianity would require sacrifice. Discipleship has its costs. But it has its rewards, too. St. John's knows that the pearl of great price is worth more than all the world's silver and gold. "You can have all the world," we like to sing. "You can have all the world, but give me Jesus."

So I knew how to present the case when Christian Peacemaker Teams asked us to send a delegation from Walltown to their project on the border of Arizona and Mexico. Ever since I'd contacted CPT's Chicago office about the local peacemaking that St. John's organized after Lil' Robert's murder, they had stayed in touch, encouraging us to get folks from Walltown more involved with CPT. I'd had to learn that CPT wasn't the answer to Walltown's problems, but I was increasingly persuaded that folks from Walltown had something to offer CPT. I wanted to take a group from St. John's and Walltown to Arizona, but I knew they would go only if they knew Jesus was calling them to make the sacrifice.

I started with Reverend Hayes. "Hey, you remember how Leah and I went to Iraq with that group of Christian peacemakers? Well, they want a group of us from Walltown to go down to the desert in Arizona. People have been dying in that desert. They want us to come down, see what's happening, and pray about what the church can do. I think God might want us to do it. But it won't be easy. Pray about it." That was all I said. Then every time I saw Reverend Hayes, I'd say, "God told you to go with us to Arizona yet?"

"When you going?" Reverend Hayes would ask.

"In August."

"How hot does it get in August?"

"Doesn't usually get above 120 degrees."

For a month, we went back and forth like this every time we saw one another. Then Joe stopped me in the street one day. "The Lord told me I need to go with ya'll to Arizona. I've never even been on a plane, but I'm trusting the Lord."

Not long after that, Reverend Hayes asked me how many bags she could bring to Arizona. I asked if that meant she was going, and she laughed and said, "I'm trusting the Lord, Jonathan!" Over the next few weeks, our neighbor Abura, Sarah from Rutba

House, and a few other friends from around Durham signed on to join the delegation. We met in the parking lot at St. John's early one Saturday morning and held hands in a circle. Reverend Daniels prayed for us as we bowed our heads, trying to get used to the straw hats we'd bought to shade us from the desert sun. When the prayer was over, Reverend Hayes pulled out a little battery-powered fan from a dollar store, held it up to her face, and called my name. She wanted me to know that she was ready for the desert. Maybe following Jesus required sacrifice, but there wasn't any need to make it harder than it had to be.

We flew to Tucson, gathered our camping gear at baggage claim, loaded up in two minivans, and drove to Southside Presbyterian Church. After a night on the floor of their fellowship hall, we got up to join the congregation for Sunday morning worship. Members of the church told us how during the 1980s they had started welcoming refugees from Central America. Because the United States supported the governments these people were fleeing from, they could not get official refugee status. As the people at Southside got to know them and prayed about the situation, though, they knew God wanted them to welcome these refugees. They declared their church a sanctuary and committed to welcome the stranger in their land.

After the North American Free Trade Agreement (NAFTA) was passed in 1994, the United States government had begun to militarize the border, increasing security at border cities to prevent migration between Mexico and the United States that had been customary up until that point. This meant that the Mexican migrant worker who had walked across the border to catch a bus before had to walk three to five days through the desert to catch the same bus now. On this journey he was liable to exhaustion in the desert heat, carrying all of his food, water, and possessions on his back. In ten years, an estimated four thousand people had died trying to cross the desert.

Southside knew that they were called once again to welcome the stranger and show mercy to those in need, so they started a "No More Deaths" camp in the desert to offer water, food, and emergency first-aid to migrants. When we gathered in worship that morning to celebrate the Lord's Supper, members of the church brought forward bottles of water and packets of food along with the bread and wine for Communion. The table Jesus invited us to was a table we shared with brothers and sisters from Mexico and Central America. To eat Christ's body and drink His blood was to remember our solidarity with people whom our country called "illegal." After Communion we ate lunch together—black, white, and brown. Then some folks from Southside gave us instructions about how the No More Deaths camp worked and sent us out into the desert.

Just before we got to the No More Deaths camp, lightning started flashing in the sky. Turns out that August in Arizona is the beginning of the monsoon season. That means it rains in the desert, and when it rains, it rains hard. Washes that lie dry and cracked most of the year fill with rushing water, crossing dirt roads and making the desert impassable. A four-wheel drive came down from the camp and someone hollered for us to throw all our gear in the back and jump on. Just as it started to rain we fishtailed our way across the muddy wash and up the hill to the camp.

As we rushed to pitch our tents, the bottom fell out. A muddy mess, we dove into tents that we hadn't even had time to stake down. I lay down, exhausted and soaked, on the already damp floor of our tent and listened to the rain beating on our rain tarp. Above the roar of rushing water, I heard Joe's deep belly laugh from the next tent over. Leah looked over at me, and we started laughing too.

We got up every morning at five in the desert, prayed together, and set out in teams to walk the desert trails with food and water. We would return to camp for rest and to refill our backpacks, making as many as five trips a day, watching and listening for travelers in distress. "Somos de la iglesia," we learned to shout out as we walked. ("We are from the church.") People crossing the desert were afraid and had learned to hide at the sound of another's footsteps. "Tenemos agua y comida." ("We have water and food.") Between the shouts, I listened to the silence of the desert and the sound of rocks sinking into the sand beneath my feet.

A couple of times, one of our groups came upon a group of migrants on the trail. Almost always they were exhausted, too tired to run for cover behind the low desert trees and cacti. We gave them water, asked if they needed medical attention, and, at their request, called the U.S. Border Control to transport them back to Mexico. Crossing the border for the sake of economic survival had nearly killed them. Now they were ready to give up the journey in order to save their lives.

When the sun went down each evening, we'd all return to camp and eat dinner together. In the cool desert evening we'd take off our straw hats and sweat-soaked socks and sit around trying to make sense of this new reality that most of us had never seriously considered. Just south of our country's border, millions of people struggled to survive in an economy where they couldn't make ends meet. The situation was so desperate that they were willing to risk their lives to walk through this desert to work jobs that practically no one in America wanted to work anyway. The law said they weren't supposed to be here, and millions of dollars had been invested in keeping them out, but they still came. And when they were picked up, shoved into cages, and hauled back to Mexico, they would turn around and come again. Joe sat staring at the ground, his jaw clenched hard as we tried to make sense of all this. He punched his fist into the palm of his other hand and spoke through still clenched teeth. "This ain't nothing but a new kind of slavery, ya'll."

I remembered Joe's words seven or eight months later when, back in Walltown, I was working in our garden one afternoon with Thomas who lives down the street from us just across from Joe. Thomas always likes to talk about the news, and one of the headlines that week was about proposed legislation to grant amnesty to the estimated eleven million Latinos who live in the United States illegally. "Well, what do ya'll think?" Thomas asked. I told him what Joe had said that night in Arizona. "It seems like these folks are in the same place black folks were in a hundred years ago. We've got an economy where a whole bunch of people have to work hard and stay poor so a little group of people can be rich. That doesn't seem right to me." I bent back over and started pulling weeds again.

"But they're here illegally, Jonathan." Thomas likes a good debate, so I kept pulling weeds and shot a question back at him: "You think the law is right?"

"I'll tell you what's not right," Thomas said. "It ain't right that we worked all those years to get a minimum wage and then these Mexicans come up here and take all the jobs 'cause they'll work for nothin'. That ain't right."

"Must mean they're getting paid even less where they're coming from," I said.

"Well, they come up here and live three families to one house. I'm telling you, Jonathan, ain't no black man gonna live three families to one house."

"We live with a whole bunch of people in one house." I was egging Thomas on.

"Yeah, but ya'll crazy!" We both laughed. "All I know," Thomas said, "is these young guys on the street ain't got jobs and they sure ain't gonna get jobs if more of them Mexicans keep coming." Maybe migrant workers were the new slaves, but the sons of the old slaves didn't seem much better off with their civil rights. They were still black, and black still meant something in America. The addition of brown slaves didn't change that. Thomas thought it made things worse.

Any African-American will tell you there is a difference between an immigrant and a slave. Immigrants came to America because they wanted to; slaves came because they were shackled, stripped, and sold, put on boats and brought here against their will. Of course, most immigrants didn't have much of a choice either. Economic and political forces pushed them to leave their homeland in search of something better. In some cases they had to flee for their lives. Nevertheless, America has been a land of hope and opportunity for the immigrant. For those who suffered slavery, the American dream always was and forever will be fraught with contradiction.

But the people who suffered chattel slavery are dead and gone. They have been for quite a while now. Still, our history of master/slave relations is always before us because America's particular form of slavery was race-based. People were not enslaved in America because of political grievance or personal debt; they were systematically selected as the cheap manual labor of a new economy in America because their skin was black. Thus "black" became a label marking bodies that were somehow different from other bodies. Though useful, exotic, entertaining, and even necessary, black bodies were not like white bodies. The ability to distinguish between black and white became an essential part of American identity.

A number of historians have written the story of immigrants to America as a tale about how a people became white. The Irish, for example, were not white when they got to America. Though their skin tone was "white" (or as white as real skin ever is), other Americans saw and portrayed them as black because they considered the Irish dirty, uneducated, poor, and uncivilized. I saw a newspaper cartoon from the early twentieth century that showed an Irishman drinking whisky on a street corner. His dress, a shamrock, and the caption all made it clear that he was Irish. But in the black-and-white color scheme of the newsprint, his skin was black. Black was a way of saying that the Irish were not yet Americans.

But the Irish eventually became Americans, as did Italians, Eastern Europeans, and Jews. All of them were "black" when they came through Ellis Island, beneath the gaze of Lady Liberty, as tired and poor immigrants to a land of opportunity. Here they would have a chance to become Americans, but only by becoming white. Those parts of their culture and identity that didn't line up with the ideals of whiteness would have to be unlearned, forgotten, and left behind. The story of millions of immigrants is a story about how people who were once part of a particular people became white in America.

The Civil Rights Movement of the 1960s questioned race-based limits on American citizenship. Millions of black Americans argued that if we say that all men are created equal and endowed by their Creator with certain inalienable rights, then we cannot have laws that institutionalize second-class citizenship for black folks. Appealing to the ideals of American democracy, the movement convinced the nation that black, white, and everyone in between deserve equal treatment under the law. Everyone must be able to enjoy the rights and privileges of being an American, no matter what the color of their skin. That's what the Civil Rights Act of 1964 guaranteed. It did not, however, question our fundamental understanding of what an American is. If the historians are right about citizenship being equated with whiteness in America, you could say that the Civil Rights Movement made it possible for anyone to become white in America—even black folks.

Another way of putting it, though, is to say that America now aspires to color-blindness. Though his fictionalized account may exaggerate to make a point, Paul Beatty's novel *The White Boy Shuffle* has a scene that captures the irony of America's post–civil rights aspirations. Early in the novel, Beatty's black protagonist, Gunnar Kaufman, recounts his primary education at a public school in 1980's Santa Monica:

> Everything was multicultural, but nothing was multicultural. The class studied Asian styles of calculation by learning to add and subtract on an abacus and then we applied the same mathematical principles on Seiko calculators. Prompting my hand to go up and me to ask naively, "Isn't the Seiko XL-126 from the same culture as the abacus?" Ms. Cegney's response was "No, we gave this technology to the Japanese after World War II. Modern technology is a Western construct.[1]

Continuing her lesson on American multiculturalism, Ms. Cegney asks the class for examples of color-blindness at work in American society. One student answers, "Justice." Another, the teacher's pet, says, "The president sure seems to like people of color." When Ms. Cegney asks Gunnar if he can think of an example of something that's color-blind, he replies, "Dogs." Ms. Cegney:

"I believe that dogs are truly colorblind, but they're born that way. Class, it's important that we judge people for what?"

"Their minds!"

"And not their what?"

"Color!"[2]

In the next scene, Gunnar is called out of class to the school's gymnasium for a free physical by city health workers. Beatty focuses on the eye exam portion of the physical:

I sat on a stool and read the eye chart with no problems. The nurse placed an open book on my lap and asked if I saw any numbers in the pattern of colored dots. I pointed out the yellow-orange eight-six in the sea of gray dots and asked the nurse what I was being tested for. The doctor stopped shaking long enough to interrupt the nurse and answer, "Colorblindness."

"Our teacher says we're supposed to be colorblind. That's hard to do if you see color, isn't it?"

"Yeah, I'd say so, but I think your teacher means don't make any assumptions based on color . . .

"So?"

"So just pretend that you don't see color. Don't say things like, 'Black people are lecherous, violent, natural-born criminals.'"

"But I'm black."

"Oh, I hadn't noticed."[3]

Like I said, Beatty hams it up a little bit. (Fellow white folks, you can stop feeling guilty. You're supposed to laugh. White guilt is the first thing black folks want us to get over.) The humor in Beatty's novel is based on a tension that is real in our post–civil rights era. We've tried to move beyond race and insist that all cultures are created equal, but we've done it without going back to question how five hundred years of racism shaped our thoughts and feelings about what is true and good and beautiful. Our ideal of the good American citizen is still shaped by the icons of Washington, Jefferson, Franklin, and Adams. Horatio Alger Jr. is still lauded for pulling himself up by his bootstraps. Einstein is still the epitome of human intelligence. Barbie is still beautiful, only now you can buy a Barbie with dark skin. Maybe because it's so visual, black Barbie is the oxymoron that defines multiculturalism's contradiction for me. Her hips, her lips, and her waist haven't changed — just her skin color.[4] Multiculturalism seems to say that anyone can become white, no matter what the color of his or her skin.

Again, "white" here means a good American — a law-abiding citizen who has a right to equal protection under the law and equal opportunity to produce and consume in a free market. So, on the white-black color caste spectrum that has defined American society, Latino immigrants have the apparent advantage of a skin tone that is no darker than their Italian predecessors. If they are willing to learn English and aspire to whiteness, they can "pass" more easily than black folks who've been here for centuries. At the same time, however, most poor Latinos are in the United States illegally. Though their skin tone may grant them an on-ramp to citizenship, their legal status is a constant dead end. A Mexican man in Walltown has to find a new job every two weeks because he doesn't have a social security number to give his employer. Even if he spoke perfect English and flew the American flag on his front porch, he couldn't vote, get a loan from a bank, or collect the social security that his employers take out of his check. Joe's right: He's a slave to the system. But Thomas is right too. If a Mexican immigrant submits himself to slavery, he does it in hope that his children will have a chance to live the American dream. He inevitably benefits from a racist system that he may not even understand. All the while, the system pits black against brown in their struggle to survive on the white man's terms.

When we were in Arizona with CPT, our delegation met with Ray. He was a representative of a group committed to defending our nation's southern border because they are convinced that the federal government is not doing enough to keep migrants from crossing the desert. These self-proclaimed heirs of Paul Revere—mostly retired white guys driving SUVs—sit out in the desert heat keeping watch and calling Border Patrol whenever they see someone they suspect of being an "illegal." They assure the media that they are not attempting to apprehend or deter migrants by force, but they carry handguns in holsters and rifles in their gun racks. I was surprised they agreed to meet with us.

We drove to Tombstone, Arizona, for our meeting. The town looked like a set from an old Spaghetti Western with tourist shops added in. Because this group of independent militiamen has bought out the local paper, a faux Wild West tabloid that they use as a platform for their anti-migrant agenda, the newspaper office is also their headquarters. We met on the back patio.

Ray greeted us by saying that he knew we were "an anarchist group committed to the destruction of America." He said he wasn't interested in being a freak show but that he wanted dialogue. Since he was already on the defensive, I tried to assure him that we, too, were there to listen and discuss the differences in our assessments of the situation. Over the next hour and a half, we did a lot of listening.

Like a lawyer accustomed to arguing a case in court, Ray was good on his feet, asking questions of the group and working from whatever answers were offered toward his ultimate point. At stake, he insisted, was the rule of law and our nation's security. He had nothing against Mexicans. As a matter of fact, he told us proudly, he was married to one. But she had come to America legally and was an upstanding citizen. Ray respected civil rights and said he had marched with Dr. King in the sixties. He was even willing to concede that the United States may need to revamp its immigration laws. But in the meantime, he said, someone must enforce the laws we have. Otherwise, the law means nothing. When we asked why he objected to our giving food and water to people who were dying in the desert, Ray insisted that we were aiding and abetting illegal aliens. We were traitors to our country, he said, and didn't appreciate the freedoms that people had given their lives to secure for us.

I began to see that, unlike the good lawyer he appeared to be, Ray wasn't necessarily going to rest his case at any point. So after he had covered the same ground a few times, I reminded him that we had agreed at the beginning of our meeting to listen to one another and try to clarify our difference of opinion. I wanted to see what he thought of this distinction. "It seems to me," I began, "that you are devoted to our country and its laws. These migrants are breaking America's law, and since you know no higher law, you believe they have to be stopped. We, on the other hand, are part of a church universal that extends across the borders that nation-states establish. Of course, we don't live in wanton disregard of our nation's laws. But when America's law conflicts with God's Law, we obey God." For ninety minutes, Ray had responded to every question or comment from our group with relentless monologue, stating and restating his case. But to this assessment of our differences, he nodded his head in agreement.

Ray had given up on God while watching his friends die in Vietnam, he said. But they had died for America, and he was determined to defend this nation as long as he lived. "It's a shame we'll never be on the same side," he said as we shook hands at the end of our meeting. I looked him in the eye and got the feeling that he almost wished we were, though he knew I could not come to where he was and he wasn't about to move. Maybe my feeling was just projection. I wished he were on my side. "You never know," I said. "It's a long story."

I grew up in America's heartland and cut my civic teeth listening to Republican tobacco farmers talk politics on the church's front porch. I understand where someone like Ray is coming from. Frankly, if all I had to go on was the story of America, I think I'd be working to halt the "illegals" at the border. (I admit I am an extremist of sorts. Convictions that folks don't act on aren't very convincing to me.) But I do believe that it's a long story I've been made part of as a Christian—a story longer than the story of America. It's a story that goes all the way back to "In the beginning."

The story that starts with Genesis is a story about how, in the beginning, God decided to create the heavens and the earth. God made a place for people to live and then made people in His image. God made us to be like the Trinity, a community of persons sharing life together. The God who is Father, Son, and Holy Spirit created women and men to join the eternal dance of life to the tune of perfect love. That's how our story begins.

But ours is a tragic story, and you don't get far into it before the perfect community God imagined is shattered by individuals' selfishness. Our built-in desire to be like God gets twisted all the way around into a decision to disobey God. Eve eats the forbidden fruit, Adam follows suit, and it isn't long until brother is killing brother. The community God dreamed of is broken, bent now toward a politics of violence. The garden where God invited people to live with Him in peace is no longer open. Cain can feel the precariousness of his situation: "I will be a restless wanderer on the earth, and whoever finds me will kill me" (Genesis 4:14).

Notice the contrast between God's hope for humanity and Cain's reality. God wanted to create a community of peace and well-being—a people whose life looked like God's life. But now Cain is alone, wandering the uncultivated spaces of a world that was created to sustain community, afraid of every encounter with another individual. Genesis says Cain's reality was so far from God's intention that "the LORD was grieved that he had made man on the earth, and his heart was filled with pain" (6:6). So God decided to destroy humanity with a flood of water.

But God didn't give up hope that people might learn to live together with Him in peace. Even in the chaos and destruction of the flood, God carved out a little space for Noah and his family to survive along with the animals that God had made humanity responsible for in the garden. Together with God in this little ark, Noah's family would learn to live the life that God had made them for—caring for the animals and depending on God for life. After the flood was over, God blessed them with the same blessing He had given Adam and Eve in the garden: "Be fruitful and increase in number and fill the earth" (9:1). God promised to never destroy the earth again. On His word, God made a covenant with Noah. God chose to bind Himself to people.

But people are tragically broken in the story the Bible tells. We don't know how to take a blessing. No sooner had God established a covenant with humanity than the people got together and decided to build a tower all the way to heaven so they wouldn't have to be scattered across the earth. They put their heads together and developed the technology to build a city that would not only bring them together but also make a name for them. The only thing that stopped them was that God confused their language. Before, Genesis says, "the whole world had one language and a common speech" (11:1), but after Babel humanity was divided into peoples that spoke different languages. This was God's judgment against the centralization of power for the sake of self-promotion. But God's judgment is also God's grace. By confusing the language of people, God initiated the formation of peoples who would check one another's power and so save humanity from self-destruction. If you want to know where peoples come from, Genesis has no race theory to offer. All the peoples of the earth exist because God had to confuse us to save us from ourselves. Babel is where peoples come from.

The rest of the story, beginning with Sarai and Abram in Genesis 12, is a story about God's plan to save the world through a peculiar people. God forms a people, brings them out of bondage in Egypt, gives them a way to live together, and promises to make them a light to all the peoples of the earth. In Jesus, our story says, God made good on His promise. Jesus fulfilled God's plan by calling women and men from every people to live as the people of God. This story says that every people will have to learn from God's people what it means to live the life we were made for, which means that our primary allegiance is to God. Our identity is not found in the peoples we come from; our identity is in the people of God, despite differences in language, skin color, or national borders. Because God has made us part of this long, long story, all other stories about who we are must be called into question. The story that says white is better than black cannot last any more than the story that says white and black Americans are better

than Mexicans. But, at the same time, the story of multiculturalism, which says that every people has something to contribute to
the fulfillment of humanity's great mosaic, isn't our story either.
The Bible says that humanity has already been fulfilled in the
body of a crucified Jew. "He's got the whole world in his hands,"
the old spiritual says. And we believe it's true. The whole world is
sitting in Jesus' nail-scarred hands. But that means we can't have
Jesus without embracing the alien and stranger whom Jesus calls
His own.

I'll admit, it's pretty hard to imagine a church where our bap-
tisms mean more than the cultures of the peoples we come from.
Multicultural churches are easy on college campuses or in the
suburbs, where people with brown and yellow, black and white
skin have all agreed to be good Americans. They already have a
common speech: the language of multiculturalism. It is the language of America, a language that has allowed for cooperation
in the production of technologies we never thought possible and
in the construction of skyscrapers that reach into the heavens,
making a name for our global economy. Despite God's judgment
against Babel, we have sought to create a melting pot where peoples would not check one another's power but rather unite their
forces for the sake of world domination. What is both incredible
and terrifying about America at the beginning of the twenty-first
century is that we have succeeded to a great degree in achieving
this goal. As I write today, a cabinet made up of white men, a
black woman, and a Hispanic man is leading the United States
in a global war on terror to ensure the continued possibility of
America's way of life. Our way of life was attacked, of course,
when men who did not believe the story of America flew airplanes
into the World Trade Center, one of the greatest towers this nation
ever built. America responded with resolve not only to rebuild the

tower but also fight back. As ardent patriots work to defend our southern border, men from St. John's are deployed to Iraq along with white boys from my home church in King. Racial divisions that the church has not been able to overcome are set aside for the sake of defending America.

The tragedy of our public life in America is that we have tried to move beyond a history of racial injustice without accounting for how race made us who we are as a nation. A friend shared with me a particularly poignant example of this predicament. Every spring in Wilmington, North Carolina, locals celebrate the end of winter and the budding of new life with an Azalea Festival. Young women put on antebellum dresses and perform the lily-white beauty of the Old South. But this is the New South, and we are trying to move beyond our embarrassing history of racism here in North Carolina. So a few years ago, my friend tells me, the organizing committee of the debutante ball decided to invite young black women to join their promenade. Now as flowers bud and hormones bubble with the new warmth of spring in Wilmington, black women have the chance to don hoopskirts and represent the ideal of a way of life in which their foremothers were bought, beaten, and raped with impunity.

Not long after my friend told me this story, I got an advertisement in the mail for a new mega-church in our town. In full color with glossy finish, the ad invited me to a church where white, black, and Hispanic worship together on Sunday morning, all in business suits and pretty Sunday dresses. The pictures seemed to say, "Anyone is welcome here, so long as you dress and act like a middle-class American." It occurred to me that this ad would not have been possible thirty years ago. Indeed, things have changed in the South. But it seems that our transition to multicultural mega-churches might be driven by the same social forces that make it possible for young black women to dress up like southern belles and white guys from farm country to fight with black guys from the inner city in a war to defend America's way of life. That white, black, and Hispanic Americans can find unity in worshipping the plantation owner's bellicose God doesn't sound like good news to me. Rather, it makes it all the more difficult to name our need for reconciliation and hear the good news of another way of life.

Another way of saying this is that the language of multiculturalism makes it harder for the church to speak in tongues. Caught up in the story of America, we forget that the Bible reverses the story of Babel not with a melting pot but with Pentecost. As my teacher Jay Carter writes, "A crucial sign of the coming of the Spirit, and therefore of human conformity to the Cross, is the ability both to hear and to speak languages that are not one's own."[5] When the Holy Spirit comes on the gathered people of God at Pentecost, the result is not a return to the one common language that people spoke before Babel. God's judgment against consolidated power and its exploitation for self-glorification remains. And yet the reconciliation that God has made possible in Jesus means that a new unity is possible. People who are made part of Christ's body by the power of the Spirit can hear and speak languages that are not our own. In Jesus, we are a new kind of people — a "non-nationalistic nation," Dr. Carter likes to say. We are a people whose borders have been opened to all the peoples of the earth.

It's sometimes hard to imagine on a Sunday morning at St. John's what it would mean for our neighbors from Mexico to be part of the worship service. Those of us who went down to the border two years ago came back saying that we wanted to make those connections — to see what it could mean for us to be

a church with neighbors who may very well have made that peril-
ous journey through the desert. But after two years, we've still
not had a single Latino neighbor join us for worship at St. John's.
What may be even worse is that I can't say I have a significant
relationship with a Latino neighbor, despite the fact that half our
block now flies the Mexican flag. If anything is going to bring us
together, it sure doesn't seem like the church is it.

But every once in a while on a Sunday morning, someone
gets caught up in the Spirit while praying and starts speaking
in tongues. This is not a planned part of the service, like simul-
taneous translation in those churches that are intentional about
welcoming non-English speakers. No, speaking in tongues is
an unplanned interruption, an outpouring of God's Spirit that
reminds us that we are not in control. God is bigger than us and
our plans.

Speaking in tongues has never been a part of the established
white church in America. People who are in power shudder at
the thought of someone "babbling irrationally" up in front of
everyone else. But the Pentecostal movement gave rise to tongue
speaking among poor whites and blacks on the underside of
the American dream at the beginning of the twentieth century.
When someone prays in tongues at St. John's, I believe it's a sign
that we haven't sold out to the powers that would unite us in
middle-class rationality against the global poor. It's a reminder
that another world is possible, even when we can't see it, where
all peoples are bound together in the foolishness of the cross.

NINE

No More Chains Holding Me

On Wednesday nights at St. John's, I teach Bible to the middle school kids. Like most kids in their early teens, they aren't particularly enthusiastic about it. I don't think it's a lack of interest in the Bible. They don't act particularly enthusiastic about anything that adults say they ought to do. But, for whatever reason, they keep showing up for Wednesday night Bible study. So we have a deal: If they read the Bible with me for an hour, I let them hang out and talk about who looks good and what song is hot and who got in a fight at school until the adult Bible study is over. Since it takes the adults about an hour to get good and going, that means I get to join in on their Bible study too.

But joining the adult Bible study midstream, I've had to learn how to pick up on a conversation that's been going on for a while. It's not always easy. You have to listen, not just to what people are saying but also to how they're saying it. And you have to read all the signs that are available. I usually glance over someone's shoulder and try to see what passage his Bible is opened to. I pay attention to body language. I watch where people point when they say, "You said . . ." or "I agree with what she was saying." I pay attention to Reverend Daniels' questions. I know I'm coming in late, so I'm slow to speak. But I'm always trying to find my way into the conversation. After all, the conversation is what I stay for.

About a year ago I finished Bible study with the kids one Wednesday night and walked over to the sanctuary, slipped into a row at the back, and started listening. People were sharing stories about the homes they grew up in. Not easy stories. They weren't the how-we-used-to-have-fun-even-when-we-had-nothin' stories that old folks in Walltown like to tell the kids when they complain about not having the newest video games. They weren't how-we-used-to-walk-to-school-uphill-both-ways stories either. These were painful stories about how Daddy used to beat Momma and how Granddaddy got drunk on white liquor every evening until the day he died. Some folks started crying as they told their stories, and someone sitting close by would lean over and hold on to them. I listened and heard people saying things like "my family's curse" and "that's what I need to be set free from."

Eventually, I gathered that the topic for the study was "generational curses": the sins of the fathers that are passed down to the children. Reverend Daniels said that if you look at the family history of an abuser, you can usually find someone who abused them when they were young. We learn our habits and thought patterns by imitation, and the people we imitate most are our families. It's how we learn who we are and where we've come from and what's important. But it's also how patterns of sin get transferred from one generation to the next. Reverend Daniels said we needed to identify the generational curses in our families, confess them, and call on the power of God to deliver us from their power. Jesus gave His life to set us free, he said. We needed to live in that freedom.

I started thinking about my family back in King and what they'd passed down to me. When they told me that Jesus loved me, I never doubted it because I knew my mom and dad would sacrifice most anything to make sure my brother and I had what we needed. From Granny Bern to Pa and Nana to Mom, my family had handed down to me a faith that I could sing. Dad performed the simple conviction that nothing in the world is more important than Jesus and His will for our lives. And my church family reinforced their witness, teaching me Bible stories and sending me off on mission trips where I learned to trust God when things were uncertain and I didn't speak the language. I knew I'd lived my life on the spiritual capital of those who came before me. But I also knew the minute I heard that phrase "generational curse" that it applied to me. Along with the gifts of my heritage, I'd also inherited a legacy of white supremacy.

Over the next few months of Wednesday night Bible study, I listened to the testimonies of people who were being delivered from generational curses. Some of them were going back and having hard conversations with family members, confronting them about things that had happened in the past. They weren't sugarcoating reality; they were speaking the truth. But they were doing it with love. They were going with tears streaming down their cheeks to pray with their mothers and fathers about addictions and patterns of abuse that had nearly destroyed them. They were claiming the power of God to break the curse before it touched another generation. They were laying hands on their grandchildren, asking God to make a way out of no way and deliver them from destruction. I noticed in the stories people told that when they experienced freedom from the generational curses of their families, it didn't mean freedom from their families. They weren't liberated from the relationships that had been broken and destructive. Their testimony was that freedom in Christ had brought them closer to their families. Mother and son were praying together for the grandchildren. By God's grace they were being set free to love one another.

I thought about how Reverend Barber had been a gift to me. Somehow I'd recognized his voice among the fragments of the faith we held in common. Even though the history of the South said that we were enemies, Jesus said that we were brothers. He preached the same gospel that Granny sang, but when Reverend Barber preached it, I'd learned that it could hurt. He had shown me how different King looked to a black man, and I'd had to rethink the way I'd learned to see the world from King. It hadn't been easy, but I was grateful for it. I was glad I'd walked away from power politics to find beloved community in Walltown. I was glad I'd learned to question the American dream so I could stop chasing an ideal up North and come back to where I'd started from, to meet Jesus all over again in the South. I was glad I'd seen the limits of multiculturalism so I could wait together with my brothers and sisters at St. John's for the new creation that only God can give.

Like every Wednesday night at Bible study, I'd come late to the conversation. But here I was, trying to read the signs and learn what I'd missed and hoping to hear what God was saying to all of us together. Sure, it was a little awkward sometimes. But I'd seen enough to know there were some things we could learn only if we were reading the Bible together. I was glad to be reading with a people who cared to name the sins that plague us from one generation to the next.

I thought about how white supremacy is a generational curse. We white folks learn it by imitation and practice it without thinking, and it makes us sick in our souls. Most of the time we're so used to being sick that we don't think we need a doctor, and we're so afraid of death that we cling to a way of living that destroys us. We're a lot like the alcoholic who grew up in the home of an alcoholic but gets defensive anytime someone suggests that life would be better without the bottle. Life without alcohol looks like the end of the world to him.

But Reverend Daniels told us that God was able to overcome generational curses, and I heard stories about the new life people had found when Jesus set them free from old patterns of addiction. One brother in the church told me, "I never knew that life could be this good." He thought that every day was just about making it through, and if a drink or a joint could help him do that, he'd take it. But since God had set him free from that curse of addiction, he'd made friends, started a family, and become part of the church. He wasn't just free from his old ways; he'd stepped into something new—something he hadn't even been able to imagine before. After the end of the world as he knew it, he discovered a whole new life.

Listening to his story, I started to realize that it was my story. Back in King I never imagined living the life we live here in Walltown. Like my brother at St. John's said, "I never knew that life could be this good." In a world shaped by white supremacy, the best thing I could hope for was becoming the president of the United States and using that position of power to do good things for those who were "less fortunate." Sure, I always wanted to be free from the stigma of being a racist. But where I came from, I couldn't have imagined a world other than the one that runs by the logic of white supremacy. (And I certainly didn't know to call it "white supremacy.") I couldn't imagine another reality beyond the world as I knew it. I guess I didn't really believe in life after death.

But that's what the gospel says — that the Creator of the world came into the world and died so there could be a whole new world. We believe in new life after death. The church has taught me all along that if I give my life to Jesus and die to my old self, God is able to give me new life. Somehow the curse had kept me from hearing how my old self was racist, tied to a death-bound social system and separated from black brothers and sisters. But God's power was stronger than the power of the curse. He died to set me free from the power of race so I could be united with black brothers and sisters in the new reality of Christ's resurrected body.

At the end of Mark's gospel, after Jesus was buried on Friday and stayed in the tomb all day Saturday, three women — Mary Magdalene, Mary the mother of James, and Salome — went early on Sunday morning to anoint Jesus' body with spices (16:1). As they were on their way to the tomb, they talked with each other about how they were going to roll back the heavy stone that covered the grave. With that question on their minds, they got to the tomb and saw that the stone had already been rolled away and a young man was sitting inside the tomb. Who was this guy? A grave robber? Since we know the end of the story, we're inclined to think he was an angel — and that may well be true — but I doubt that's the first thing those women thought. Mark reports that they were scared to death.

But the young man said, "Don't be alarmed. You are looking for Jesus the Nazarene, who was crucified. He has risen! He is not here. . . . But go, tell his disciples and Peter, 'He is going ahead of you into Galilee'" (Mark 16:6,7). To some women whose worlds have just been shattered, this is the message of good news: Jesus is going ahead of you into Galilee. He is not here, where you hoped to find Him. The best you knew to hope for was a dead man to honor, a corpse to anoint. But the One who was dead is risen. Only, He is not here—He is going ahead of you.

Jesus has gone ahead to Galilee, back to the world that His disciples knew best (the world they were sure to return to). Now these women are supposed to tell the rest of the disciples that their Master has overcome death and inaugurated a new world. It is a world they can live in if they will trust the promise of God and follow after One whose existence they can't yet imagine. "He is going ahead of you into Galilee," Mark says. That is the message of resurrection hope that Mary, Mary, and Salome bear.

What does this peculiar story of resurrection hope have to offer a church divided by the history of race in America? I've been learning with the saints at St. John's that this is the story that tells us who we are. Mark's resurrection story invites us to reimagine ourselves as disciples on the way to see our resurrected Lord. What if we are those women whose lives have been shattered because the one hope we thought we had has been crucified? If that is who we are, then our hope is decidedly not in the long march of history toward the ideal multicultural civilization. Neither is it in a heaven that floats above the earth, promising real life only after this world is over. No, our faith is in a Master who got up from the dead and has gone ahead of us to Galilee. He's gone ahead of us, back to the place we started from. If what these women say is true, there is one who has defeated the power of death by submitting to it and trusting the Creator of all things to remake Him. He is risen, and there is a power in the universe stronger than the intertwining logic of race, multiculturalism, and death. To be disciples is to find our identity in pursuit of a risen Savior and the new world He embodies.

One Sunday morning in the midst of our study on generational curses, Sister Daniels testified that she saw a new future for the church. St. John's wasn't just a black church anymore. Things were changing, she said. We needed to get ready. God was about to do a new thing. She doesn't say that sort of thing often, so I took notice.

A few months later, at the beginning of 2006, there was a new banner at the front of the church: "Called to the Ministry of Reconciliation, 2 Corinthians 5:18." Reverend Daniels preached about how God was calling us to be ambassadors of reconciliation so that people who saw our life together would see the power of God to break down dividing walls. Throughout Black History Month, our Wednesday night Bible study was about forgiveness and the power of God to overcome offenses. Then came March, Family Month at St. John's. On the last Sunday of Family Month, members are encouraged to invite their family and friends. The sanctuary is always packed as the church clerk reads off each family and asks them to stand with their guests. Grandmothers beam at the sight of their clan dressed to the nines in front of the whole church.

But this year the tradition was interrupted. When the time came for the parade of families, Sister Daniels got up and started talking about Sarah and Abraham. She told the story of how God called one family and promised Abraham that through his family all the peoples of the earth would be blessed. She said that because of Jesus' blood, we have become part of God's family. Our last names didn't matter and the color of our skin didn't matter because we'd all been adopted into Sarah and Abraham's family.

Then, instead of calling each family by name, Sister Daniels asked us to hold hands and sing the song that says,

I need you, you need me.
We're all a part of God's body.
Stand with me, agree with me
You are important to me
I need you to survive.

As we sang, I looked around the sanctuary at the faces of people I hadn't known three years before. They were brothers and sisters I had never thought of until I heard the gospel from Reverend Barber. But here we were together. They were my family. I looked out at all of them as we held hands and swayed to the music. And I caught a glimpse of what it looks like for God to set us free from the bondage of a racialized history to be bound to one another in community.

St. John's is not a perfect church, and I don't think we have all the answers to America's race problem. But ever since that service on Family Day, I've been thinking about how God has given us a new identity by liberating us to live and worship together across the color line that has defined American identity. Our common history in this country has enslaved us in different ways, but it has enslaved us all. You might say we've suffered different generational curses. Some of us have been held down by discrimination, and some of us have been prisoners to power. Some of us have been addicted to crack, and some of us have been addicted to money. But God has set us free for life together. We have been called out from our different cultural identities to be one new people. We are a people on our way to Galilee. We are pilgrims together in pursuit of God's new world.

St. Augustine said of the church that we are a people "on the way," headed toward the new reality of God's city even as we travel through the cities of this old world that are passing away. I think that's true of the church at St. John's. We haven't made it to the City of God yet, but we're finding our way together. And because we're together, we already have a new identity in the world. We're not a black church. We're not a white church. (And we're certainly not a multicultural church.) We're a new kind of church. Maybe you could say we're a church on the way.

But another of the saints, Catherine of Sienna, said that "all the way to heaven is heaven because Jesus said, 'I am the Way.'"[1] So if we're the church on the way, we're also already the body of Christ. It's a mystery, I know. But it's a mystery with flesh on it, which means that we can touch and see it. From this peculiar place where we live in America, I see every day the residual and sometimes quite overt effects of white supremacy. I would like to defeat that racism by any means necessary. But I have come to believe that most of the means we generally employ only reinforce the assumptions that give rise to race in the first place. At St. John's, though, as I have learned to know black women and men as sisters and brothers in Christ. I've seen the power of Christ's resurrection to give us an identity that is more fundamental than the color of our skin in a racialized society. The only proof the church has for this new reality is our love for one another. "By this," Jesus said, "all men will know that you are my disciples, if you love one another" (John 13:35). We do not have a blueprint for what a new world of peaceful and just relationships with one another will look like. We do not know for sure how we will survive in a world yet conditioned by the logic of race. But we know that the only place where we will have the power to figure these things out is in the resurrected body of Jesus. And He is going ahead of us into Galilee. So we follow the lead of the women — Mary, Mary, and Salome — and chase after God's new world, assured that our identity as disciples offers us a better hope than the cultural identities we are leaving behind. We believe in life beyond death — a new life in which we're free to be bound.

Discussion Guide

Chapter 1: I'll Fly Away

1. Jonathan tells a story of growing up in the Bible Belt, saturated with Scripture and familiar with Jesus. Dissatisfied with "otherworldly" religion, he tried to put his faith into practice through politics. How have you tried to make faith real at different times in your life?

2. Martin Luther King Jr. said that 11 to 12 a.m. on Sunday is the most segregated hour of the week in America. Half a century after the integration of public schools, this might be even truer. Why do you think the "color line" is so strong in American churches?

3. The very idea of racial *re*conciliation implies that there was a time and place when black and white were not divided. Is this true? Where do we look for hope that the gospel is stronger than the power of race?

4. Wendell Berry argues that beyond the separation of white and black bodies, race created other dividing walls—between mind and body, faith and politics. Where do you see these divisions working themselves out in

Jonathan's story? Have you felt the same divisions in your own life?

5. Why does Jonathan write that Reverend Barber spoke from "a world I would have to die to enter into"?

Chapter 2: If It Had Not Been for the Lord

1. How would you describe your church culture? Have you had experiences where you felt like a "fish out of water"? Did they help you see something new about the water you're used to swimming in?

2. What does the experience of "falling out" reveal about the world that black Christians live in?

3. Why does Jonathan call the existence of the black church a miracle?

4. Jonathan tells the story of how he saw his home through Reverend Barber's eyes and realized that he was from "Klan country." Jonathan had never seen the Klan in action, but he also had not grown up with black folks. How does a history of racial division continue to shape our experience in post–civil rights America?

5. If white is not just the color of some people's skin, what is it? What does it mean to be white?

6. Jonathan tells the story of the Southern Baptist Convention's statement concerning the submission of women as an example of how a history of race shapes the way white Christians read Scripture. Are there other interpretations of Scripture that you think race has influenced?

Chapter 3: I Need You, You Need Me

1. Jonathan presents European high-culture and the gospel of reconciliation in Christ as two alternatives to the racism of

Klan country. Why are these two not the same thing? Why does Jonathan think conversion is a more promising antidote to racism than education?

2. In college Jonathan felt called to downward mobility, while his black roommate, James, wanted to work for economic empowerment. What did they learn from each other about how their different experiences as black and white affected their sense of God's calling?

3. Why isn't it enough to say that "all cultures are created equal"? Does multiculturalism subtly reinforce racial divisions?

4. Could white and black churches justify our separate existence without believing that we are somehow culturally different—and that cultural difference is okay?

5. If the story of a cultural melting pot is not able to overcome racism, how is the story of God's covenant with Abraham and Sarah different? What is the scandal of God choosing a peculiar people? What is the good news?

Chapter 4: Nobody Knows but Jesus

1. Reconciliation requires relationship, but Jonathan talks about learning how relationships between black and white folks are so often built on mistrust and lies. What else is required for real reconciliation? How can peoples who are divided by a history of injustice learn to trust one another?

2. What doubts did Jonathan and Leah have about whether they could be part of a black church? What made them feel uncomfortable? Have you felt uncomfortable in cross-cultural worship experiences?

3. What does Jonathan mean when he says that Saint John's asked him to become black? What is "blackness"? Can white

people choose it? Should they?

4. How does Jesus affirm our identity when He calls us to discipleship? How does He challenge it? What would humility like that of the Canaanite woman look like in your life?

Chapter 5: I Want Jesus to Walk with Me

1. Jonathan recounts the painful experience of being lied to by Jerry. Have you had experiences like this? What does Jonathan mean when he writes about the "bigger lie" of economic inequality that they had not addressed at Rutba House? Is it possible to talk about racial reconciliation without talking about money?

2. How was the conversation the Rutba House had with Raymond about moving to Walltown similar to the conversations Jonathan had with James in college? Are there ways the conversations were different?

3. What does the story of Moses teach us about exploitative economies and how God saves the people of Israel?

4. Jonathan writes about the questions that couldn't be asked when he and the Rutba House moved to Walltown. Do you have questions you don't feel you could ask people of another race? What are they?

5. Jonathan writes about how Raymond moved from being guest to host when the Rutba House relocated to Walltown. What made this possible?

Chapter 6: I Know It Was the Blood

1. Jonathan tells the story of Lil' Robert's murder in Walltown and the way the local churches responded. What did Jonathan learn from Reverend Daniels and Reverend Hayes? What wisdom do you see in their response?

DISCUSSION GUIDE

2. Do you hear apocalyptic language in your church? Do you hear other Christians use it? How does it make you feel?

3. Why do you think Jonathan, who believes in Christian nonviolence, wants to take Nat Turner so seriously? Why should white people listen to black anger?

4. What do you think it would look like if black and white Christians, together with others, lived out the prophetic tradition of black Christianity? Where have you seen a need for this kind of Christian witness? Have you seen it embodied?

5. How does Mamie Mobley invite us to see the world around us through the blood of Jesus? Where does Jesus meet her? Where does He meet you?

Chapter 7: Climbing Jacob's Ladder

1. Think about the role the church has played in the black community. How does it compare to the role church plays in your community?

2. Jonathan writes about feeling lonely with his questions about how the church could welcome William. What are the fears that kept him from talking with his pastor or fellow church members about this? What did he learn when he did talk with Reverend Daniels about it?

3. What kind of church did W.E.B. DuBois dream of? How did Urban Hope live out DuBois' vision in Walltown? What was missing from DuBois' vision?

4. What does Jesus teach us about the way God's kingdom comes on earth? What difference does that make for churches that want to make a difference in their communities?

5. Who does Jesus say we are as Christians? What claim does

197

race have on our identity?

6. What is the goal of church life? Where are we going together? What does baptism show us about how we get to where God wants us to be?

Chapter 8: The Whole World in His Hands

1. What difference does it make if your ancestors came to this country as an immigrant or as a slave? How does this affect conversations about race and ethnicity?

2. What does it mean that many immigrant groups "became white" in America? What does this show us about whiteness?

3. If our primary identity is with the people of God, what does that do to national allegiance? Who are your people?

4. What does the story of Babel teach us about the origin of peoples and nations? Does this story help you rethink ethnicity in any way?

5. What hope does Pentecost offer us in a world where different peoples and languages intersect in neighborhoods, schools, and churches?

Chapter 9: No More Chains Holding Me

1. How is racism like a generational curse? Have you experienced race as a curse?

2. Imagine what life would look life if you were free from the power of race. What would you have to leave behind?

3. To whom are you free to be bound? Are there people you share life with because of Jesus whom you would not be bound to otherwise?

4. Mark's gospel says Jesus is going ahead of us into Galilee. What is the next step on the way for you? What might the next step be for your church, small group, or ministry?

Notes

Chapter 1: I'll Fly Away

1. Albert J. Raboteau, *Canaan Land: A Religious History of African Americans* (New York: Oxford, 2001), 19.
2. Wendell Berry, *The Hidden Wound* (San Francisco: North Point Press, 1989), 16.
3. Dante Alighieri, *The Portable Dante* (New York: Penguin Books, 1995), 399.

Chapter 2: If It Had Not Been for the Lord

1. Albert J. Raboteau, *Slave Religion: The "Invisible Institution" in the Antebellum South* (New York: Oxford, 1978), 4.
2. Frederick Douglass, "Slave Holding Religion and the Christianity of Christ," in Milton Sernett, ed., *Afro-American Religious History: A Documentary Witness* (Durham, NC: Duke, 1985), 104.
3. Minnie Fulkes (former slave), in Albert J. Raboteau, *Slave Religion*, vii.
4. Henry Wiencek, *The Hairstons: An American Family in Black and White* (New York: St. Martin's Griffin, 1999), 234.

5. Transcription courtesy of Chewie World Order, http://chewok.blogspot.com.
6. Raboteau, 175.
7. Howard Thurman, *Jesus and the Disinherited* (Richmond, IN: Friends United Press, 1981), 13.

Chapter 3: I Need You, You Need Me

1. Eric J. Sundquist, ed., *The Oxford W.E.B. DuBois Reader* (New York: Oxford, 1996), 102.
2. Immanuel Kant, "What is Enlightenment?" in *Perpetual Peace and Other Essays on Politics, History, and Morals*, trans. Ted Humphrey(Indianapolis: Hackett Publishing, 1983), 41–48.
3. Zora Neale Hurston, *Mules and Men* (New York: Harper & Row, 1990), 13.
4. Martin Luther King Jr., "I Have a Dream" in Clayborne Carson, ed., *The Autobiography of Martin Luther King* (New York: Warner Books, 1998), 224.

Chapter 4: Nobody Knows but Jesus

1. Heather Christine Deutsch deserves credit for digging up the details of this history for her master's thesis, "Walltown: The History of a Neighborhood and a Housing Renovation Program," submitted to the faculty of the Department of City and Regional Planning of the University of North Carolina at Chapel Hill in 2004.
2. Deutsch.
3. Kelly Brown Douglass, *The Black Christ* (Maryknoll, NY: Orbis Books, 2004), 18.
4. James H. Cone, *A Black Theology of Liberation* (Philadelphia: J. P. Lippencott, 1970).

5. James H. Cone, *God of the Oppressed* (New York: Seabury Press, 1975), 241.

Chapter 5: I Want Jesus to Walk with Me

1. Robert Screiter, *The Ministry of Reconciliation* (Maryknoll, NY: Orbis Books, 1992), 89.
2. Howard Thurman, *Jesus and the Disinherited* (Richmond, IN: Friends United Press, 1981), 58.
3. Michael O. Emerson and Christian Smith, *Divided by Faith: Evangelical Religion and the Problem of Faith in America* (New York: Oxford, 2000), 113.
4. Emerson and Smith, 132.
5. Charles Hurst, *Social Inequality: Forms, Causes, Consequences* (Boston: Allyn and Bacon, 1998), 147.
6. This comparison is based on the median net worth of blacks according to data from the Survey of Income and Program Participation, as cited in Emerson and Smith, 13.
7. John Perkins, *Let Justice Roll Down* (Ventura, CA: Regal, 2006), 48.
8. Perkins, 62.
9. Perkins, 185.

Chapter 6: I Know It Was the Blood

1. John McCann, "Cycle of prayer vigils, violence," *The Durham Herald Sun*, July 14, 2004. My memory of this whole series of events was aided by the good coverage of this local columnist who came out and joined us for prayer walks in Walltown on more than one occasion.
2. Marva J. Dawn, *Powers, Weakness, and the Tabernacling of God* (Grand Rapids, MI: Eerdmans, 2001), 4.

3. Scritti di Christofono Colombo, ed. C. de Lollis, Roma, 1894, II, pt. 1, "Libro de las profecias," 76. I am indebted to Delno C. West's paper "Wallowing in a Theological Stupor or a Steadfast and Consuming Faith: Scholarly Encounters with Christopher Columbus' 'Libro de las profecias'" for both this quote and the summary of Columbus's work that follows. The paper was delivered at the First San Salvador Conference, October 30–November 3, 1986, in San Salvador Island, Bahamas.

4. Carol Delaney, "Columbus' Ultimate Goal: Jerusalem," *Society for the Comparative Study of Society and History, 2006,* 28.

5. Nat Turner, "The Confession of Nat Turner," in Milton Sernett, ed., *Afro-American Religious History: A Documentary Witness* (Durham: Duke, 1985), 91–92.

6. Turner, 99.

7. I am indebted to Ryan McCartney's article in the *Duke Chronicle*, "NAACP Leader Calls for Solidarity, Action in Troubled Times" for all quotes from the chapel service and prayer gathering. See *The Chronicle Online* at http://www.dukechronicle.com/media/storage/paper884/ news/2006/04/05/News/Naacp.Leader.Calls.For.Solidarity. Action.In.Troubled.Times1783814.shtml?norewrite20061102 1138&sourcedomain=www.dukechronicle.com.

8. This story and the direct quotes are taken from Charles Marsh, *God's Long Summer: Stories of Faith and Civil Rights* (Princeton, NJ: Princeton, 1997), 18–24.

9. Eugene Rivers, "The Idol of Whiteness," *Sojourners,* March–April 1997, 30.

10. Studs Terkel, *Will the Circle Be Unbroken?* (New York: The New Press, 2000), 393.

11. Studs Terkel, 394.
12. Studs Terkel, 396.

Chapter 7: Climbing Jacob's Ladder

1. W.E.B. DuBois, "Of the Faith of the Fathers," in Eric J. Sundquist, ed., *W.E.B. DuBois Reader* (New York: Oxford, 1996), 203.
2. DuBois, 207.
3. DuBois, 207.
4. DuBois, 207–208.
5. W.E.B. DuBois, "The Revelation of St. Orgne the Damned," in Herbert Aptheker, ed., *The Education of Black People: Ten Critiques, 1906-1960* (New York: Monthly Review Press, 2001), 148.
6. DuBois, "The Revelation," 149.
7. DuBois, "The Revelation," 148.
8. Ralph Ellison, *Invisible Man* (New York: Vintage Books, 1995), 576.
9. Ellison, 580.
10. Ellison, 577.

Chapter 8: The Whole World in His Hands

1. Paul Beatty, *The White Boy Shuffle* (New York: Owl Books, 1996), 29.
2. Beatty, 30–31.
3. Beatty, 32.
4. Willie Jennings taught me to see the whiteness of Barbie's beauty, along with many of the other contradictions of multiculturalism that I've tried to point out. Endnotes usually tell the reader where the author got an idea or a quote. I'm aware that almost everything I'm saying in this

chapter—and much of what I've said in the rest of this book—I learned from Willie Jennings. He taught me "Black Church in America" and "Doctrine of Creation" at Duke University's Divinity School. If he ever writes a book, you should read it.

5. J. Cameron Carter, "Race, Religion, and the Contradictions of Identity," *Modern Theology* 21:1 (January 2005): 57.

Chapter 9: No More Chains Holding Me

1. Quoted in Robert Ellsberg, *Dorothy Day: Selected Writings* (Mary Knoll, NY: Orbis Books, 2002), 104.

Author

JONATHAN WILSON-HARTGROVE is a graduate of Eastern University and Duke Divinity School. An associate minister at the historically black St. John's Baptist Church, he speaks and writes frequently about Christian hospitality, peace-making, and discipleship and is actively involved in reconciliation efforts in Durham, North Carolina. The Rutba House, where Jonathan lives with his wife Leah and other friends, is a new monastic community that prays, eats, and lives together, welcoming neighbors and the homeless.

Jonathan directs the School for Conversion (newmonasticism.org), an alternative seminary that offers courses at new monastic communities around the country and study circles on Christian practices in Durham, North Carolina. He is associate editor for the Resources for Reconciliation Series, a partnership between Duke Divinity School's Center for Reconciliation and InterVarsity Press. Jonathan is also the author of *To Baghdad and Beyond: How I Got Born Again in Babylon* (Cascade, 2005), *Inhabiting the Church: Biblical Wisdom for a New Monasticism* (Cascade, 2007) and *New Monasticism: What It has to Say to Today's Church* (Brazos Press, 2008). His articles have appeared in *PRISM, The Other Side, Radiant, The Christian Century,* and *The Raleigh News and Observer.*

Check out these other titles from NavPress.

The God Who Smokes
Timothy Stoner
ISBN-13: 978-1-60006-247-6
ISBN-10: 1-60006-247-4

Perhaps no recent spiritual movement has caused more division than the emergent church. For some, the trend represents a refreshing resistance to fundamentalist attitudes. For others, the ideas suffer from a lack of sound theology. Is there a middle ground? With a casual, narrative voice, Timothy Stoner presents an honest look at a controversial subject.

Between Two Worlds
Mike Timmis
ISBN-13: 978-1-60006-248-3
ISBN-10: 1-60006-248-2

What motivated an evangelical-based ministry to choose this Catholic as its chairman? Mike Timmis's inspiring life as a Catholic and evangelical leader reveals how our unity in Christ transcends the two worlds' differences. From him, we learn how Catholics and evangelicals can go into an alienated world together as ministers of reconciliation and witnesses to God's salvation and love.

The End of Religion
Bruxy Cavey
ISBN-13: 978-1-60006-067-0
ISBN-10: 1-60006-067-6

In *The End of Religion*, Bruxy Cavey contends that the Jesus described in the Bible never intended to found a new religion; instead he hoped to break down the very idea of religion as a way to God. With a fresh perspective on biblical stories, Cavey paints a picture of the world God originally intended and still desires: a world without religion.

To order copies, visit your local Christian bookstore, call NavPress at 1-800-366-7788, or log on to www.navpress.com.
To locate a Christian bookstore near you, call 1-800-991-7747.